Unseen Worlds

by the same author

The Spiritual Dimension of Childhood
Kate Adams, Brendan Hyde and Richard Woolley
ISBN 978 1 84310 602 9

of related interest

The Creation of Imaginary Worlds
The Role of Art, Magic and Dreams in Child Development
Claire Golomb
ISBN 978 1 84905 852 0

A Child Sees God
Children Talk About Bible Stories
Rev Dr Howard Worsley
ISBN 978 1 84310 972 3

Children and Spirituality
Searching for Meaning and Connectedness
Brendan Hyde
ISBN 978 184310 589 3

Chasing Ideas
The Fun of Freeing Your Child's Imagination
Christine Durham
ISBN 978 1 84310 460 5

The Spirit of the Child
Revised Edition
David Hay
With Rebecca Nye
ISBN 978 1 84310 371 4

Unseen Worlds

Looking Through the Lens of Childhood

Kate Adams

Jessica Kingsley Publishers
London and Philadelphia

First published in 2010
by Jessica Kingsley Publishers
116 Pentonville Road
London N1 9JB, UK
and
400 Market Street, Suite 400
Philadelphia, PA 19106, USA

www.jkp.com

Copyright © Kate Adams 2010
Printed digitally since 2011

Library of Congress Cataloging in Publication Data
A CIP catalog record for this book is available from the Library of Congress

British Library Cataloguing in Publication Data
A CIP catalogue record for this book is available from the British Library

ISBN 978 1 84905 051 7
ISBN pdf eBook 978 0 85700 243 3

**154.
3
ADA**

Contents

Acknowledgements

This book would not have been possible without the help of children who chose to share their experiences and ideas with me, as well as the children I have never met myself, but who shared theirs with other researchers cited in this book. One of the most gratifying aspects of undertaking research with children with whom I have no prior acquaintance has been their openness and willingness to talk and share with me – a stranger. Children have consistently reported that they have not previously told anyone about their experiences. Sadly, this theme is echoed in other research of a similar nature yet all these children need is an adult who has a genuine desire to know about these aspects of their inner lives, who will respond with respect and without judgement. I have been privileged to have been one of those adults. My sincere thanks also go to their head teachers, class teachers and parents/carers who granted me permission to invite children to talk to me, for without their informed consent, as well as that of the children themselves, then the child's voice simply cannot be heard within a research context.

Similarly, I am indebted to the adults who graciously shared their childhood recollections of their unseen worlds. Their willingness to talk openly about issues which they would not normally discuss, and how their experiences impacted upon their lives, has been very much appreciated as it teaches us pertinent lessons about how we should respond to children. Ultimately it is only through the willingness of these adults and children to disclose their experiences that others may be able to understand children better when they talk of worlds which can remain unseen to many others. For ethical reasons, all of their names and other identifying features have been changed.

I am also grateful to those friends and colleagues with whom I have had many inspiring and challenging conversations about various aspects of my work, and different people have played a variety of important roles in the creation of this book. I thank Brendan Hyde who was present when I first started to make notes on the structure of the book during a sabbatical in Australia, and whose friendship has remained throughout the writing of it. Thanks also go to Howard Worsley for the very challenging and thought provoking conversations about my work which he initiates. From the earliest days in my role as a researcher of children's significant dreams, I have been inspired by the work and encouragement of Kelly Bulkeley, and I also thank Roger Knudson for demonstrating the immense value of qualitative research methods which illustrate the impact of significant dreams upon an individual. My gratitude also goes to Jennifer Parker for her passionate commitment to children, their imagination, creativity and insights and for her support for this book. Time is so valuable, and writing a book requires so much thinking and writing time, that it inevitably impinges on relationships and to that end I have to thank various people for their responsiveness to that situation. Janet and John Dennett continued to show wonderful friendship and a sensitive approach to the pressures on my time whilst I was writing it. Similarly, thanks go to Becky Bull for her recognition of my time commitment to the book and also for her delightful ability to see the world through the lens of childhood, which echoes a key theme of this book that encourages us to temporarily suspend the adult filters through which we see the world. My parents have also continued to be sympathetic and supportive of my commitment to this book, as indeed, throughout my life, they have been supportive of the professional paths I have chosen to take. This book could not have been written so quickly had it not been for my employers at Bishop Grosseteste University College Lincoln who granted me a sabbatical in order to write it. I am highly indebted to all the staff who were involved in that decision, and particularly to Graham Meeson who has shown constant support and appreciation for my research and for whom it is an absolute pleasure to work. Finally, I thank the staff at Jessica Kingsley Publishers for their commitment to publishing this book and their unfailing support and attention to detail throughout. They are a delight to work with.

Preface

Unseen Worlds is a journey into the realms of childhood which many of us once made ourselves but have long forgotten, or at least only have hazy memories of. It is a voyage into the calm and enchanting worlds which children inhabit alongside, and intertwined with their daily lives of school, work, family and social life: worlds of fantasy play, imaginary companions, seeing deceased loved ones, of travelling into strange worlds in dreams, to name but a few. But it is also a journey into the somewhat turbulent worlds which children move in and out of: fearful worlds of monsters hiding in their cupboard and the creatures chasing them in their nightmares.

The book came into being after many years working as a primary school teacher and then as an academic in the education sector where I have supported students in their quests to become educational practitioners in a variety of settings, working closely with children. Over the decades researchers have provided invaluable insights into the minds of children and there has been a growing appreciation and understanding of the wider elements of children's lives, such as their emotional, social, cultural, personal, physical and spiritual development and a current and increasing emphasis on their health and well-being. Practitioners in all environments working with children are rightly concerned with these personal areas of children's lives and are aware of the importance of building strong relationships with the children with whom they work in order to facilitate and nurture these many aspects of children's growth.

It might, therefore, be safe to say that professionals who work with children understand children, not simply based on strong theoretical foundations, but also through their regular interactions and developing relationships with them. Yes, we have gained much knowledge from research, theory and practice about how children develop cognitively, emotionally, morally and socially, but do we *really* understand children? Do we *really* understand how children see and experience the world? I am not convinced that we do, as well as we might. Instead, a complex interplay of cultural factors and adult filters tend to dominate and lead our responses to children, which often consist of smiles, comments or thoughts pertaining to the vividness of their imagination. This book has stemmed from a desire to explore that question after becoming aware, through my own earlier research, and reading that of others, that many children do not share certain aspects of their childhood for fear of ridicule or of not being believed. If children hide many of their experiences, then adults will of course be less aware of them and subsequently not understand children as well as they might.

In an attempt to explore how children perceive, experience and make sense of their inner worlds, I have conducted my own research over the course of three studies. The first two comprised 106 interviews with children aged 9–12 about significant dreams and the third consisted of interviewing 40 children aged 4–11 about their wider experiences and beliefs about unseen worlds. Alongside these studies, I have also conducted interviews with adults and drawn on a wide range of other international studies. This book is multidisciplinary, deliberately drawing on research in different fields in order to weave together an overview of children's worlds. Although I draw on developmental psychology, I do not approach this book from a standpoint of distinguishing between fantasy and reality or of imagination. Instead I aim to understand the child's point of view so that adults can understand children more fully, by raising awareness of the adult filters through which we see children's lives and how they affect our interpretation of their experiences. This book does not lay any claims as to the possible 'reality' of the children's experiences in the objective sense, for example as to whether or not a child's imaginary companion actually exists, or whether or not a child's deceased grandmother appeared to them. That is for the readers to discern. Instead, the text aims to convey the reality of the children's unseen worlds as they experience them; to hear the children's accounts of them so as to understand these worlds through the lens of childhood.

Dr Kate Adams
Lincoln, UK
November 2009

CHAPTER 1

Living in multiple worlds

When Sarah, a teacher in her 40s, was asked to describe one memory which expressed how she experienced the world during her childhood, she shared the following tale:

> For my brother and me, the garden was a completely separate world from our house, school and the local neighbourhood. It was a place where we could escape our parents. It had large old trees and paths which were gateways to other dimensions. The path which went in between the vegetable patches was out of bounds for many months as there was an invisible force-field which we weren't able to break through. As we approached it we would feel a strange tingling sensation and sometimes we could actually touch the force-field for a fleeting moment. We were always tempted to see what would happen if we tried to walk through it but we thought we might find ourselves transported to a parallel universe. The notion was in part intriguing but also frightening, so we decided not to try to go through it... just in case...
>
> Sarah, aged 42

Do you remember what it was like to be a child? You will no doubt be able to recall your favourite toys, the places you lived, fights with brothers and sisters, occasional memories of being at school, emotionally charged events, or family holidays by the sea. As adults, most of us have encountered those excruciating experiences of our parents pulling out old photographs of us to show relatives or new partners – our first school photograph, our beaming smile with no front teeth... Somehow it often seems that this picture is of someone else who bears a vague physical resemblance to us. There may be a disassociation with that image. Were we ever really that tiny? Were we ever really that naughty that we embarrassed our parents so much? Were we ever so shy that we wouldn't speak to anyone on our first day at school?

On our journey to adulthood, our memories of childhood will inevitably fade. We may subconsciously reconstruct our youth as we decry bad behaviour of children throwing tantrums in the supermarket, saying 'I was never like that!' A teacher may stand in front of a classroom of children and despair at how lack of respect for adults has risen so dramatically since they were young, when no one ever dared answer a teacher back, or not do as the teacher asked. But why do we, as parents/carers or adults working or intending to work with children, need to recall our own childhood? As Gabriel (2005) observes, our own childhood memories affect the ways in which we think and interact with children to a much greater extent than we may realise. He asserts that our own memories of being a child remain a vital part of who we define ourselves as now and how we think we once were. However, it is not simply the case of remembering the past for, as explained below, the concept of childhood is considerably more complex.

This book invites you to recall what it was like to be a child. But rather than encourage you to focus purely on the physical and emotional memories of places and people, instead its focus is on engagement with the self and the ways in which we perceived and perceive the world. Our recollections of places and people are naturally one vital component. For those who had a stable, loving home life and a wide network of friends, the world was a considerably more welcoming place than it was for those who had a traumatic home life, had few friends or were bullied at school. Whilst acknowledging these aspects of children's physical, social and emotional worlds, this book also puts forward the argument that children live simultaneously in multiple worlds: worlds of magic and mystery which often stand in stark contrast to their parents' world which seems dominated by mundane daily routines. These worlds are more numerous and at times more complex than simply believing in fairies and talking teddy bears and many continue to exist beyond the first four or five years of our life. Whilst adults are comfortable with young children's engagement in such 'fantasy' worlds, this book shows how they can continue to exist for older children too but often remain largely hidden from view.

Adults who work with children on a daily basis have a good understanding of the children with whom they work. Through training, experience, professional development and self reflection, practitioners gain strong understandings of how children learn and how they develop cognitively, socially, morally and emotionally. Those working regularly with the same children have a good understanding of what it is like to be that individual child, becoming aware of their socio-economic backgrounds and other influences from home and from peers. With the extensive information about children available to adults today, professionals benefit from a rich understanding of young people on many levels. But to what extent can adults claim to be able to *empathise* with children's inner worlds? Can they really see the world(s) through children's eyes?

Whilst some of these children's worlds are indeed magical, creative and imaginative, like that of Sarah, this book does not dwell on the romantic version of childhood, espoused by Rousseau, that children were born innocent and in early life should be protected from negative societal influences (Gabriel 2005). This book also recognises that some of the worlds which children inhabit are dark and potentially frightening. These worlds – of monsters and nightmares – are inescapable yet are too easily dismissed by adults who place them in 'the too-hard basket' and move swiftly on. But these shadowy worlds exist alongside the lighter, inspirational ones, and need to be acknowledged in order to gain a fuller picture of children's worlds and to help children manage and understand them constructively. Before embarking on the journey into these multiple landscapes, which will often be told in the children's own words, we need to first consider theoretical views about childhood which will enable a wider perspective than can be gained by simply recalling our own past. We start with the worlds which are at the forefront of the minds of adults, before exploring the complexities of 'childhood' and childhood worlds.

The worlds of adults

Adults' perceptions of the world are, of course, partly defined by cultural values, as anthropological studies illustrate. For those living in contemporary Western industrialised nations, life may be dictated by work, whether it be paid, unpaid caring or child rearing, household tasks or the anxieties of job-seeking. For those in full- or part-time paid employment, daily routines are often characterised by tight schedules; rushing to get to work on time; answering the influx of emails and telephone calls; attending meetings; juggling priorities; doing jobs which others want done yesterday; sitting in traffic jams; rushing to collect children from the child minder; and panicking that only two things have been crossed off the 'to do' list but six have been added. Whilst evenings and weekends theoretically bring time to rest, relaxation can be harder to find in reality. Tired from the week and with shopping and other domestic issues to deal with, opportunities for social life and recreation can be reduced.

The immediate worlds of adults are, of course, varied and are not simply defined by work, having many more facets. For those in industrialised societies, some stay at home looking after children; some are single parents; many struggle financially; some are unemployed and do not enjoy material luxuries; some are homeless and depend on shelters, hostels and charities for food and warmth. On other levels, adults' lives are also defined by their varied roles, as grandmother/ grandfather, mother/father, sister/brother, aunt/uncle, niece/nephew, friend, lover, carer, colleague etc. In non-industrialised communities, life continues to be dominated by matters of survival at the most basic form – building shelter, catching and growing food, and caring for the young, sick and elderly.

Naturally, throughout the world, adults' lives are all determined by issues of survival to some degree, but the dominance of socio-economic and material worlds in the West (and increasingly so in societies which have rapidly developing economies) does not exclude adults' engagement with other worlds. Perhaps the most common type of other world for adults, characteristic of all societies, is that with a religious and/or spiritual dimension. Here, worlds may be characterised by a belief in a divine creator, belief in an afterlife and in other ethereal beings such as angels or spirits. These realms can be inhabited simultaneously alongside the material world. This applies equally to different types of society. The Australian Aboriginal Narranga-ga tribe believe that whilst dreaming, the human spirit leaves the body to make contact with other spirits, including those of the deceased (Mallon 2002). Such beliefs in the unseen live alongside the community's practical considerations such as finding food and shelter, and are often interwoven in non-industrial communities. Similarly, belief in what may be termed the unseen is also prevalent in industrialised societies where major world religions live side by side with secular communities and those who believe in supernatural entities but do not align themselves with a religion.

What is childhood?

Before comparing the worlds of children with those of adults, it is necessary to consider the concept of childhood, for as theorists have shown, this is a vast and complex area. It is also a key area addressed by most training courses for those seeking qualifications in all areas of child-related professions. Defining childhood is a multifaceted task, requiring engagement with a range of interdisciplinary approaches. Waller (2005) observes that in Western countries the dominant discourse has centred upon developmental psychology which argues that children progress through given stages which lead them into adulthood. Piaget's (1929, 1951) developmental theories form a fundamental part of vocational courses for those intending to work with children, but more recent literature has critiqued the rigidity of such developmental theories, and interdisciplinary studies have shown how the notion of childhood is considerably more complex. As James, Jenks and Prout (2006) state, childhood is in part defined by physiological and biological factors, but there are also other factors impinging upon its definition. These include, for example, social constructions, the social spaces in which children live and changing perceptions throughout historical eras.

Ariès (1960), taking an historical perspective, highlighted the element of social construction, arguing that the concept of childhood was created in Europe in the fifteenth century when societies began to separate the lives of children from those of adults. When schooling became compulsory in the late nineteenth century, a socially constructed division was made clear (Clarke 2004, Waller 2005). Whilst Ariès has been criticised for his methodology, his work has continued to be influential, with the historical approach demonstrating how societal developments influence changes in thinking. Waller (2005) notes how economic, political and demographic factors can lead to shifts in how societies change their ideas about childhood. He offers the example of how economic conditions in the West since 1945, and the raising of the compulsory schooling age to 16, contributed to the creation of a new 'teenage' culture which had not previously existed.

Thurtle (2005) further elucidates the complexities of social definitions of childhood, arguing that societies at different times in history have viewed children in varying ways – as innocent and in need of protection, as being out of control, as investments in the future in need of sacrifices from parents, or as consumers. Indeed, at times, these views can be held concurrently and it is important to note that ideas about childhood will continue to change.

The social construction of childhood is not, however, purely defined and influenced by adults, with a range of authors exploring how children are also involved in constructing their own childhood. Waller (2005) provides an overview of contemporary thinking which emphasises the concept of agency – children's ability to understand their world and act upon it. Children are not simply individuals but also active participants in a wide range of meaningful social interactions.

A key factor in child's agency is the increased importance which has been given to hearing the child's voice, which stands in stark contrast to the historical position of Victorian middle-class children in Britain who were to be 'seen and not heard'. In 1989 the United Nations Convention on the Rights of the Child (UNCRC) attempted to improve the living conditions and experiences of children on an international scale. It outlined rights for children which encompassed protection, provision and participation rights. The latter, a new focus, included the right of children to participate in decisions for which many countries subsequently legislated. The emphasis on the child's voice has been evident in a wide range of areas of social and public policy, including issues of health, public care, education and child protection where children's views have been sought in formal contexts (further detailed in chapter 6).

Thus, children are now able to not only voice their opinions, have their opinions sought, but also to have them acted upon. This allows children the opportunity to negotiate their own childhood to some degree, considerably changing the balance of power between adults and children compared to a century earlier. For example, the media and advertisers have now created a consumerist culture amongst children. Thirty years ago, children wanted toys, sweets or comics just as they do now, but money was in less supply. Today, with more disposable income and/or high levels of borrowing and debt, and more sophisticated and expensive products on the market, children have been targeted as consumers. But these products are not simply more sophisticated and expensive; many are sold as 'lifestyle accessories'. Young girls seek clothes once deemed more suitable to teenagers and children want mobile phones to chat with their friends. Waller (2005) notes the recent creation of 'tweenies' – 7- to 12-year-olds who show teenage tendencies, largely through such consumerist choices. As Kehily (2003) notes this group has considerable spending power of their own and as a result have ranges of products specifically directed at them, some of which are branded as lifestyle choices and include make-up and even cosmetic surgery. A result is a blurring of the distinction between children and teenagers. Thus many children are actively negotiating their own childhood, expressing what they think defines it, including a right to choose, a right to demand material goods and a value placed on the importance of visual appearance.

Whilst we might initially see childhood as a simple concept, it is clearly a multi-faceted phenomenon and, as with all theories, each of those outlined above has been critiqued. Such discussions are held in depth elsewhere (see Mooney 2000; Wyse 2004; Taylor and Woods 2005; Waller 2005; Willan, Parker-Rees and Savage 2005). This brief overview here highlights the complexity of defining and understanding childhood and acts as a reminder to adults to be aware of their own definitions and assumptions about it. It is important as professionals and as parents/carers that we explore our own underlying notions about children and consider them in terms of historical and cultural contexts in the widest sense of their meaning. These assumptions which we hold, which may be partly subconscious, will affect how we interact with children and how we respond to their ideas and experiences. As will become apparent in this book, the ways in which adults respond to children who share their multiple worlds can have a significant impact on young people, and thus have longer-term consequences for the dynamics of their relationships and the children's sense of self. These multiple worlds take many different forms and some are much more visible than others. So what might these seen and unseen worlds look like?

Children's seen worlds

For children around the world there is a wide range of socio-economic factors which determine their immediate worlds. Poverty, work and mortality are key issues in many countries. The World Health Organisation (WHO) highlights the contrasting mortality rates of children aged five years and under around the globe. In 2004, they estimated that for every 1000 live births, 5 children in Australia would die, 6 in the UK, 8 in the USA, compared to 85 in India, 117 in Haiti and 283 in Sierra Leone. The importance of basic factors affecting health, lifestyle and survival cannot be overstated, even for some children living in Western countries, living in relative poverty and/or neglect and abuse.

These socio-economic worlds which are highly visible are thoroughly explored by other authors (see Taylor and Woods 2005, Willan *et al.* 2005) whilst this book enters the multiple worlds of children beyond those defined by material circumstances, and focuses primarily on children living in the West with some reference to children in non-industrialised societies. Whilst most of these multiple worlds are unseen, some are partially discernable to the observer. The most obvious example is that of fantasy or role play, in which children adopt the persona of other characters and act out scenes inspired by observations of adults' behaviour, television programmes, stories and imagination. For adults there is no doubt that these children are participating in two parallel worlds, which do not conflict with each other, and the creative worlds of play are explored in depth in the following chapter. However, other worlds remain largely unseen to the naked eye.

Children's unseen worlds

Unseen worlds co-exist alongside these more visible worlds of the socio-economic and of play, as exemplified by Andrew, a solicitor in his 30s, who recalled his childhood journeys to school. 'We used to have to walk approximately half a mile to get there,' he explained.

> My mum would walk behind me talking to her friend while I would run on ahead. I would be completely absorbed in my quest not to tread on any of the cracks in the pavement which separated the paving stones. I had to jump and hop and alter my pace to make sure I didn't. But I had to avoid the cracks. If I jumped on one I knew that would condemn me to a day of bad luck because my brother had told me that treading on them meant that you had killed a fairy. I laugh at that now of course, it just seems so ridiculous. But for a few years I really believed him and I was scared of having the other fairies take revenge on me if I killed one of them. At the time no one could have convinced me that my brother was lying to me.

Andrew's tale is useful for exemplifying the nature of the term 'unseen' as used in this book. The term refers to elements of children's worlds which adults do not see, or do not fully understand in the ways in which the child does. To Andrew's mother, he was playing a game which involved not stepping on the cracks. She was not aware of the whole narrative for three reasons. First, Andrew's action of avoiding the cracks in the pavement simply looked like a game and did not suggest that he had any particular role as he would have done had he been pretending to be a pirate or racing car driver and been acting accordingly. In this case, his role of trying not to tread on fairies was hidden from view. Second, the world of the fairies was invisible to Andrew's mother because she could not see it, despite the fact that she had done so when she was a child. Finally, the fairy world remained unseen in that Andrew engaged with it privately. In this case, he did not articulate his interaction with it to his mother.

Andrew's story offers a good example of the contrasting perceptions of the worlds of adults and children. As an adult, he is now a firm non-believer in fairies, which lies in opposition to his belief in them as a child. Yet as a child it wasn't simply that he believed in the existence of fairies, as many children do: there was more substance to it. Instead his daily journey to school was actually influenced by this belief, determining every single step he took on the road to and from his destination. Andrew, like many adults, can remember and articulate the way in which he perceived the world as being different to how his parents did. But at the time, when he was six years old, this was a very real conviction that there were other worlds operating in parallel with his daily world of home and school. There was an authentic 'land of fairies' interacting with the physical world seen by adults, and Andrew was a part of both worlds. Had Andrew's mother been aware of his beliefs about the fairies, she would most likely have labelled it a land of make-believe or imagination. Indeed, that would be the dominant cultural view of the West, and one to which Andrew as a mature man now subscribes. However, for 'Andrew the-six-year-old' this was a very real world; one which was so real that it influenced his actions on a daily basis. This meaning given to unseen worlds by children is essential for practitioners to acknowledge and understand. Sometimes the worlds offer children pleasure and happiness, at other times they inspire awe and wonder or trepidation… sometimes they give meaning to children and serve as inspirational moments which can remain in their memories into adulthood. Sometimes children will describe them as imaginary but sometimes they perceive them to be very real. But above all, many children make meaning from this engagement with other worlds – meaning which often goes unrecognised by adults.

Adults' lenses

Adults are often bemused, entertained and enchanted by the things children say. Young children particularly are smiled at sweetly and commented on as being cute as they make their observations about the world and ask questions of people around them. In their early years, children are particularly expressive of these other worlds as they dress their teddy bears and feed them, wait for the tooth fairy to replace their lost tooth with a gift and eagerly await the delivery of presents from Santa Claus as he flies around the world in one night to give presents to every well-behaved child.

The place where adults' understanding and acceptance of these multiple worlds is most evident is in the pre-school, nursery/kindergarten age group. In formal play settings, the layout of the room and resources are visible affirmations of young children's participation in these worlds of magic and make believe. Indeed, adults actively encourage children's involvement in them: the 'dressing-up' corner allows children to engage in fantasy or role play, where they take on different characters and different lives for short periods of time; building blocks and construction toys allow children to create new places to inhabit; teachers regularly alter parts of the room to create a doctor's surgery, a café, a shop, or a hospital, so that children can take on others' roles; story corners display books filled with cartoon animals which can talk, tales of children flying to other planets and fairies granting wishes.

Practitioners in early years' settings have a particularly heightened awareness of how children perceive these worlds, in part due to their training and in part due to young children's lack of inhibition in displaying their involvement in them. As the following chapter details, young children's participation in symbolic play, which is well documented in psychological and educational literature, is an outward and accepted indication of their active involvement in other worlds. But chapters 3 and onwards take readers beyond these widely-accepted worlds of children's play to illustrate the wider variety of worlds which exist and, importantly, show how these worlds are relevant to children over the ages of six or seven. Research, which will be detailed later, shows that societal pressures and taboos influence children at a relatively early age. Children quickly become aware of topics which are deemed acceptable to talk about and those which are not. There comes a time when children realise that they are 'too old' to believe in Santa Claus and that such a fanciful idea is something for 'little children' to believe in. Likewise, children feel that they can no longer talk about the friend who sits next to them at the dinner table – a friend who is invisible to others – for it is, apparently, only 'mad' people who see things that most people cannot.

On hearing stories of invisible friends and fairies, adults often respond swiftly, labelling them as a product of the child's imagination. Indeed, imagination it may well be, but a key point emphasised throughout this book and articulated by the children themselves, is how *real* these worlds are to the children. It is that 'realness' which can give these worlds significant meaning to children. Whilst lecturing on this topic to trainee teachers in Australia, one student said to me 'I had no idea that ten-year-olds either had these kinds of experiences or had such strong convictions about them.' This lack of awareness was unsurprising; as a student teacher she had interacted with many children on her placements and taught a wide range of lessons. But as she was unaware of the wide variety of children's experiences, she had not asked children about them or noticed them. In turn, the children were aware of society's taboos and had not initiated conversations, so a cycle of silence is born and maintained. The silence has important implications for both adults and children, and can have a significant bearing on the quality of their relationship in addition to affecting the children's self-esteem.

For all those working with young people, good relationships are a vital part of being an effective practitioner. Parker-Rees (2005) emphasises how all forms of work with children demand highly developed communication skills, including those between adults and children. These, he argues, require an ability to express ourselves clearly together with the ability to engage with the more playful modes of social conversation. A key characteristic of a good relationship is empathy, a concept which is central to Carl Rogers' (1969) person-centred theory. Rogers' theory was pioneered in the context of counselling but has also been applied to educational settings. In his work, Rogers emphasised the importance of being able to see the world through the clients'/pupils' eyes. In the following decade, Goleman (1996) popularised the theory of emotional intelligence, drawing on the work of Salovey and Mayer (1990) who provided a definition of the term 'emotional intelligence'. The concept includes the ability to empathise as well as the ability to manage relationships; these cannot be completely effective if participants cannot manage emotions in others. Empathy is a key theme in this book because it can, if sufficiently developed in the context of the adult–child relationship, take the relationship to a deeper level. Rather than simply being able to understand various aspects of children's development, such as the cognitive, social or moral, which training successfully enables, empathy will enrich the relationship further. How that empathy can be developed in relation to understanding children's worlds is detailed throughout this book.

The reflective reader

This book requires readers to be as reflective as possible. Self reflection is a key element of being an effective practitioner, a notion strongly influenced by the works of Dewey (1933) and Schön (1983). Loughran (2002), writing about teachers, suggests that among the skills needed to be an effective, reflective educator is the ability to question taken-for-granted assumptions. This principle can be applied to all interactions with children with regards to their worlds, because the underlying notions we have about childhood can influence our responses to children's expression of them. As later chapters will show, a lack of self reflection in this area can inhibit the development of empathy with children. Being self reflective requires a strong degree of open-mindedness (Pollard *et al.* 2002) but if practitioners are able to do this, then it can enable 'a shift in attitude to events, relationships and values in professional life' (Bolton 2006, p.75). By being open to children's experiences, many of which remain hidden from adults beyond the early years, educators will be able to change their assumptions about this aspect of childhood and alter and enhance their professional relationships with children.

Alongside the need to be reflective about one's own ability to recall the past, lies a need to be open-minded about the children's experiences which are detailed in this book. Some will not resonate with personal encounters and may, therefore, be especially challenging. This book deliberately uses the children's voices where possible to emphasise the ways in which the children interact with these worlds and reflect upon their experiences. In so doing, adults can gain a greater insight into them and become increasingly empathic.

Conclusion

Throughout the book, examples of the worlds which children inhabit are drawn upon. Some of these accounts may trigger memories of your own childhood which you have not been able to recall whilst reading this chapter. Others will challenge your own perceptions and beliefs. It is important to recognise and acknowledge your responses to them, for these will indicate how you may react to children who choose to share these worlds with you. Would you be able to empathise? Would you inwardly giggle and comment to your colleagues on how sweet the child was? Would you think, 'oh, it's just her imagination' and move swiftly on to another topic? Or would you explore the child's thoughts with them with a genuine desire to know more about them?

This book presents a range of worlds, though by no means an exhaustive list, including those characterised by play, imaginary friends, fairies, angels and ghosts of deceased relatives, as well as more unusual phenomena. But unseen worlds are not all magical. In fact, some are darker places where frightening creatures lurk in the shadows. Such issues of a potentially unsettling nature must be confronted, for childhood is far from a romantic tale of friendly genies in bottles and talking animals. It is, however, through the process of becoming aware of the unsettling aspects, and by being empowered to engage with them *with* the children that we can help children to come to terms with their fears and understand them. Practical guidance is given in later chapters to support you in your personal and professional roles.

Empathy with children's worlds should not be impossible to achieve. After all, every reader of this book was once a child themselves. However, the processes of growing older, of undergoing biological, cognitive, psychological, social, emotional and physiological development, of taking on new roles in life, all lead to an inevitable distancing and detachment from our own childhood. Memories will not be accurate. As Gabriel (2005) points out, they may be partially constructed by how our parents remembered us as children, by how we may have wanted our childhood to have been, or may be influenced by recent books we have read or films we have seen. Again, it is important that you analyse these other societal factors to deconstruct your own, often subconscious, beliefs which the book guides you through.

Unseen Worlds argues that beyond the early years of children's lives, adults often do not recognise the different worlds which children continue to inhabit, sometimes through the rest of their primary school years. The reasons for this lack of recognition are multi-faceted and ultimately lead to a cycle of silence. Yet these worlds are often valued by children, and are very real to them. Some worlds give meaning and significance to their lives whilst others cause anxiety. By becoming increasingly aware of the types of worlds and the impact they have upon children, adults will be better placed to understand children. This process will move readers beyond understanding children's skills, interests and personality traits to developing more empathy with them, enabling them to see these worlds as children see them. In so doing, relationships with children can be deepened.

In leading you through this argument, this book will take you on journeys which may help you to understand children in a new and more insightful way than you have to date and will support you in temporarily suspending the adult filters through which we see childhood. The following chapter takes the first step in these travels by detailing those which are familiar to adults – the worlds of play. These are of course partially 'seen' worlds given their outward expressive nature, and are the ones which adults most easily relate to, thereby allowing you comfortable access into the first of the several worlds which children inhabit.

CHAPTER 2

Worlds of play

Memories of our own childhood play can be tinged with nostalgia, as we recall the hours in which we were lost in fantasy worlds where we had powers of time travel, of becoming invisible, and of saving the world from invasion by creatures from outer space. We lived in private worlds of making dens and inventing codes to pass on secret messages. We created new worlds that were better than the ones we lived in on a daily basis. We transformed our bedrooms into dangerous places filled with monsters or pirates, played chasing games with other children and board games with the adults who cared for us. Whilst playing occasionally led to arguments and tears, it was basically fun – so much so that we often did not want to go to bed at night because we would rather be awake and playing.

Play, according to Western perceptions, is a fundamental and defining characteristic of childhood. It tends to inspire a sense of freedom which has largely been squeezed out of adults' busy, hectic lives which have to focus on work. Of course, adults still make time to 'play', whether it be with children or through sport or computer games, but childhood play seems to retain a sense of enchantment and fond memories. Margaret, a 66-year-old housewife and mother recalled her childhood play which bore similarities to that of today's children. She remembered playing Monopoly, hopscotch, taking the doll's pram out for a walk and playing marbles on the corner of the street.

In contrast, Jack, a 78-year-old retired scientist could remember little about his childhood other than significant events such as being in his father's workshop at the age of nine and hearing the Second World War being declared on the radio. With regards to leisure activities, Jack remembered playing marbles in the gutter and spending time at the nearby riverbank with three or four other boys. The riverbank play space had its own story attached to it. As a young boy, his mother regularly took him in a pushchair across a river bridge. Jack would look down at the water and was terrified of it – a fear which remained with him until he was ten years old. Then, one day, he surprised his mother by asking 'Can I go swimming with Ted?' Assuming that the swimming would be supervised, his mother agreed, unbeknown that Jack and his friends were playing unattended in the river. Whilst Margaret and Jack's examples are not of engaging in other worlds *per se*, they do embody the ways in which children become absorbed and lost in worlds of play, often occurring out of adults' sight.

Learning through play

Like all aspects of human behaviour, play has become the object of academic study and theorisation which has resulted in a vast literature. Since the 1870s, its study has focused predominantly on the cognitive, emotional and social value of play (Cohen 2006). Researchers have been keen to dissect, identify and categorise its different forms, resulting in a plethora of literature. Lindon (2001), in a chapter on theories about children's play, lists 20 types of play drawn from various academics' work, which include practice, symbolic, ludic, social, creative, object and locomotor play. Lindon also notes that such terms can denote different things by different authors and practitioners, thus illustrating the complexity of the discussions. Most theories examine the benefits of play and common foci include how it enables learning and the development of skills. The works have combined to form strong foundations for professionals working with young children. Indeed, many educational systems have designed curricula for the early years that are centred on play, underpinned by academic theory.

The benefits of play are immense and the theoretical understanding of it is well documented elsewhere (see Cohen 2006). Rather than repeating those summaries, this chapter draws on research and theory to explore play in a way that focuses more specifically on the worlds which children inhabit during it. Whilst attention will be given to academic studies, I argue that there is a danger of over-theorising play, where it can become a vehicle for learning skills, thereby losing the naturalness and spontaneity which is naturally inherent in it. In such a process of formalising play, adults can take away the richness for the child who is simultaneously living in a world that is only partially seen by the adult observer.

Play, play and more play

Throughout history and across cultures, children have played and adults have watched and/or taken part. Jaffé (2006) suggests that toys have always been an integral part of children's lives. Archaeologists have discovered marbles dating back from the Stone Age, and children in Ancient Greece, Rome and Egypt played with dolls, spinning tops and balls. In Europe, the Middle Ages saw the creation of the hobby horse and model knights on horseback and the eighteenth century witnessed the manufacture of the first dolls' houses in Germany. As Lindon (2001) also notes, some toys in historical and cross-cultural contexts also had spiritual significance too. For example, in the European Middle Ages, coral teething sticks were added to babies' rattles because coral was believed to contain supernatural powers that would ward off evil as well as prevent gums from bleeding.

As Jaffé (2006) observes, all around the world, children who do not have purpose-made toys will improvise with objects around them whether it be using a stone as a ball, or a pebble as a spinning top as it skims across the water. Children's use of toys and props is a visible example of how they create their own fantasy worlds, which often involves them using symbolic thinking. In symbolic play, a twig is no longer a twig, but a gun to shoot the armies advancing over the hill; the plastic bottle is no longer a bottle but a microphone for the latest pop star to sing into; and the paper cone is no longer a cone but a hat which once worn makes the wearer invisible. Children appear to have a natural disposition towards using symbols in play, with Bruce (2001) observing that babies are natural users of them, with a common example being that of a very young child using a doll to symbolise a baby.

Another type of play is role play during which children pretend and imagine scenarios which may or may not involve the symbolic use of toys or props. Here, they adopt roles of other people and imitate their actions, for example by playing the role of a doctor or a vet. Bruce (2004, p.187) gives an example of Michael who, in a nursery school setting, combines this with imaginative play as he drives his bus to Italy after visiting the travel agents which the practitioners had helped the children to construct. Michael's bus is a large mat and he uses plastic blocks for the pedals and handbrake. Michael invites other children and staff onto the bus and as his friend passes by in his car, Michael shouts 'Hi mate!' and winks, saying, 'That's what drivers do!' Role play can be an expression of children's explorations of their identity. In many cases they are mimicking adults around them as Margaret, mentioned at the opening of this chapter, recalled. She lived in Liverpool where her aunt worked at a local button-making factory and brought home reject buttons for Margaret and her friends to play with. Margaret had a toy cash register and used the buttons as coins as she assumed the role of shopkeeper.

Fantasy worlds

Fantasy play – which can also involve role play and symbolic play – transports children into the worlds where anything can happen and they can be anyone or anything they want to be. They develop a sense of self as they take risks, explore and create. Here there are no boundaries to the worlds in which they can live; literally anything is possible. Adults will be able to see some of the visible signs of this type of play as children dress up or act out their alter egos. In the group of 4- to 11-year-old children I spoke to about their play, a wide variety of imaginary characters and worlds were brought into being. Kitty, aged five, loved to pretend to be a puppy while Megan, aged seven, enjoyed dressing up as a witch. The influence of the media was clear amongst most of the children. Several were particularly fond of Mr Benn, a character created by David McKee who appears in books and a television series. Mr Benn wears a suit and a bowler hat and is seen each day leaving his house and stopping at a fancy dress shop. There, he tries on an outfit and leaves the changing room via a magic door which transports him into another world, appropriate to the costume he is wearing, where he has an adventure. The children I spoke to were captivated by Mr Benn's ability to travel to other worlds and sometimes emulated him. Connor aged five said:

'We go into a wizard world and do magic.'

'Can you do magic there?' I asked.

'Yeah,' said Connor.

'Not real magic with us, like Mr Benn can do,' Finn intervened.

… 'Mr Benn can travel to any worlds,' said Connor.

Other media influences included films. A group of six-year-old boys enjoyed re-enacting scenes from the films *Star Wars* and *Toy Story*, with a particular emphasis on using guns and other weapons to kill invading aliens. In these imaginary worlds of play, they could become their own heroes and superheroes and take charge. Adventure was a key theme to their activities, which continued with the older children who had been inspired by the magical land of Narnia, created by C. S. Lewis (Lewis and Baynes 2006) and became a place to visit in their own play.

In a more unusual but intriguing type of fantasy play, some children invent what Silvey and MacKeith call 'paracosms' (Cohen and MacKeith 1992). Paracosms are imaginary worlds which children create (but are not to be confused with 'imaginary companions' which are explored in the following chapter). Singer and Singer (1990) describe paracosms as elaborate private societies or alternative worlds, and note that they have rarely been studied.

One of the earliest recorded cases was the creation of worlds by the authors the Brontë sisters, Charlotte, Emily and Anne, and their brother Branwell. After receiving a set of toy soldiers from their father in 1826, Charlotte and Branwell were inspired to create Verdopolis, the great Glass Town, which later became the country of Angria. The children showed immense focus and attention to detail as they created numerous characters and documents such as poems and chronicles for the world. Later, Anne and Emily created their own world of Gondal. Letters written by the girls showed that these worlds remained with them into adulthood, as a passage which Charlotte wrote at the age of 20 illustrates:

Never shall I, Charlotte Brontë, forget how distinctly I, sitting in the school room at Row Head, saw the Duke of Zamorna leaning against the obelisk... I was quite gone. I had really utterly forgot where I was... I felt myself breathing quick and

short as I beheld the Duke lifting up his sable crest, which
undulated as the plume of a hearse waves to the wind.
                                        (Cohen and MacKeith 1992, p. 4)

Cohen and MacKeith (1992) go on to present a range of paracosms
drawn from some of the 57 adults who described their own from
childhood. The depth of detail and creativity of many of these worlds
is remarkable, particularly because some started as young as the age
of three, although most began between the ages of seven and 12.
One example was that of Kate who entered Petsland which had been
created by her ten-year-old brother, when she was seven. It comprised
three cities with the larger toys living in Petsville, the medium in
Juville and the small ones in Hamville. The first president was a large
teddy bear called Edward Smythe-Holand who eventually ended up
in prison after becoming alcoholic. Being arrested was unusual in this
land as crime was quite rare because the citizens were often in high
spirits and hard-working. One teddy bear was a gifted businessman
who eventually created a merchant bank. Petsland came to an end
three years later when her older brother eventually outgrew it.

Children's creation of such sustained, highly detailed paracosms is
a relatively unusual form of play in which other worlds are visible to
the observer, but is nonetheless a fascinating one which completely
absorbs the architect.

The changing worlds of children's play

Play is inevitably influenced by the culture in which a child lives, and
thus as a culture changes, children's play can be affected. The most
startling change seen in some Western societies in recent years is the
gradual decrease in outdoor play and the accompanying increase in
indoor play. Jenkinson (2001) notes the range of societal factors in the
UK that have taken many children off the streets where they would
once have played, and into their homes. These factors include a more
risk-averse society which has left many public play areas sanitised.

Parental fears of child abduction, fuelled by media reporting of
a small number of cases, have further led to children being ushered
indoors, despite the fact that statistically children are no more likely to
be abducted than they were 100 years ago. Jenkinson (2001) further
suggests that the UK's roads are now filled with cars, which replace the

children who once played in them, making them dangerous. Concerns are expressed that children are now spending too much time indoors at the expense of time spent playing outdoors (Waller 2007). With interesting parallels, Weber and Dixon (2007) observe the historical changes in the USA where children freely played unsupervised on the streets of the early twentieth century, creating their own private spaces. Half a century later, adults began to create commercial playgrounds and organised clubs such as boy scouts where they brought children's play under control.

Of course, such a move towards indoors play is not applicable to every country. Punch (2000) studied a rural community in Bolivia where children's lives are centred on school, play and work. The work is essential to the survival of the household, involving tasks such as herding animals, scaring birds away from crops and fetching water. The work and school aspects of their lives dominate, severely restricting their time for play, but nevertheless many children actively create their own play spaces. Their opportunities for doing so are enhanced by the lack of fear for personal safety that overshadows many Western societies, and they are allowed to freely roam the surrounding countryside and mountains, with the only safety fear relating to the strong river currents in the wet season. Children tend to walk to school unaccompanied by adults, and some use this opportunity to play, occasionally making them late for lessons or even not attending, unbeknown to their parents. Many children also arrive home late because of creating time for play after school. Their favourite locations for play are the football pitch and in the community square (although interestingly the adults think that the children favoured playing at home). A gender divide is observed in the choice of activity, with boys preferring football and marbles and girls finding *chasquitas*, a plant with long thin leaves, which they plaited to look like dolls' hair.

In the more affluent countries where children have been driven inside to play, another change has been witnessed in the types of leisure activities. Here, the rapid rise of relatively low-cost but sophisticated electronic media has brought new worlds into the living rooms and bedrooms of millions of children. The worlds of televisions, DVDs, the Internet, mobile phones and computer games lie in stark contrast to the childhoods of the 1940s and 1950s. I spoke to Maureen, now in her late 60s, who said 'Science fiction? Oh no, we had no concept of time travel so there was no playing of those kind of games. There was no such thing as Doctor Who back in my childhood. Life was very unsophisticated and quite simple then.' In contrast, Veen and Vrakking (2006, p.5) describe today's children as 'homo zappiens', – children who are born with a computer mouse in their hands and who are natural users of technology.

Reflecting on the changes in children's play

Some aspects of children's worlds of play such as the indoor nature of digital and cyber play have clearly altered, but it is important to reflect carefully on a range of issues when we consider how children have been affected. This process can help adults elucidate their thoughts about children's play which can in turn affect their interactions with children, albeit subconsciously.

The digital-related changes in play are echoed in other industrialised countries, where popular culture appears to blame technology for robbing 'children of the capacity to enjoy the sort of imaginative outdoor play which adults recall from their own childhood' (Holloway and Valentine 2003, p.119). The increased use of computer-based play combined with other factors such as unhealthy diets and lack of exercise have led to widespread concern about the increasingly sedentary nature of childhood. For many children, particularly those who have access to technology at home, their worlds are certainly different to those of our childhood, and with regards to worlds of play, new opportunities are available to them.

Jenkinson (2001) laments the rise in electronic toys, claiming that the repetition of the games leaves children with little space to be creative and original, instead allowing them opportunities to only repeat what has been done before. Yet Veen and Vrakking (2006) argue that this is not the case. On the contrary, they suggest that the children who play computer games which simulate war scenarios are displaying the same imaginative skills as those who used to play cowboys and Indians in the past.

Weber and Dixon (2007) propose that cyber play and physical play have a blurring of boundaries, and that children create play spaces for themselves, demonstrating an ability to move freely between them. They conducted longitudinal, ethnographic studies and found that children were able to move swiftly between different types of play and also incorporate some aspects of one into another. For example, two boys, Rowan and Tucker, were observed playing in a secret place near their home where they spied on the girls who lived nearby, taking with them pieces of plywood from which they constructed forts. As rain began to fall, they moved indoors and started playing their favourite videogame about a man who had crash landed on a planet and has thirty days in which to recover the parts of his space ship and return home. Weber and Dixon (2007) noted how the boys used this virtual play space of the planet in similar ways to the play in their secret hideout, and sometimes used the outdoor space as the space ship from the videogame. Weber and Dixon argue that cyber play and physical play are not separate entities – the boundaries are hazy and children have a large role in constructing their own play.

The intertwining worlds of play

It is not simply the case that the boundaries between cyber play and physical play are indistinct, but also that the boundaries between children's play and their work (whether it be school work, paid work, or unpaid work such as herding animals, tending crops or caring for family members) are also hazy. Children, like those in Bolivia, will spontaneously find time to play and will merge in and out of the play worlds.

It is of course adults who create a distinction between work and play, and introduce this to children very early in their lives. In Western countries, children start formal schooling at different ages, from around four to seven. Most curricula in the early years are focused on learning through play, but children can quickly realise that adults set time aside for 'work' and separate time for play. This is particularly evident through the construction of the school day being divided into lessons and playtime (or 'recess' in the USA and Australia). Simultaneously, most children see how work dominates their parents'/carers' lives, whether it be household duties, voluntary work, paid employment or the search for it. But although the word 'work' enters children's vocabularies early, this does not necessarily construct boundaries between work and play, especially in their early years. As the Bolivian children showed, many will simply make spaces for themselves, sometimes playing whilst they work and at other times in between work spaces. The construction of time for play is often spontaneous as one can see when observing children walking in the street alongside adults. When conversation is not taking place between them, children will naturally be inclined to pick up items they find on the pavement with which to amuse themselves or start playing hopscotch or imagination-based games. As soon as the adult begins to talk to them, the child is able to switch back into the everyday demands and just as easily re-cross the boundary back into the imaginary world as quickly as they had left it.

Playing and empathy: recalling our childhood

Many adults join children in their play activities on a regular basis, whether it be in a work setting such as a nursery, classroom, therapeutic setting or in a social setting such as a home, garden or play centre. These situations can trigger our memories, as Bernard, a 34-year-old social worker, realised whilst playing with his friends' daughter. They were making buildings out of blocks when Bernard remembered a time when he had built a toy castle out of plastic construction materials. His older sister was playing with him and started to change the castle into another type of building. Bernard recalls being 'devastated' even though he knew that his sister only had good intentions, namely of spending time with her younger brother. He explained, 'at that time, as a child, that model was my world and she just dismantled it in front of my eyes'.

Bernard's story is a good example of how adults and older children can over-direct play, and also of how important it is to be empathic towards children's play. To the adult, creating a castle with a child might be an entertaining means of gaining knowledge about different parts of a castle and developing construction, teamwork and social skills – all of which are inherently valuable aspects of the activity. For the child it may well also be an entertaining means of learning new things, but for some children, this will be an absorbing activity which takes them away from their daily activities and immerses them in a land of castles, knights, princes and princesses. The escapist and creative elements can be particularly meaningful and any externally imposed changes or directions can be an upsetting intrusion.

Recalling our own childhood can be more difficult than first imagined. Some people may only be able to recapture occasional glimpses of their childhood play whilst others may have more substantial memories. The processes by which our memory works are complex and can affect not only how much of our childhood we can remember but also how accurate those memories are. In the final chapter, I will draw on psychological research into memory to elucidate the complexities further. In the meantime, as the chapters progress, make mental notes of any memories that arise. The more that adults can identify with children from their own personal experience, the greater the empathy can be.

Some recommendations

- Play is a partially visible world in which children can lose themselves in fantasy and imagination, into which you may be invited.

- Be sensitive when playing with children. As Bruce (2001) notes, playing peekaboo can cause a child frustration if they cannot physically obtain the object which is being hidden from them. Be sensitive to children's emotions and needs.

- Whilst play provides children with immeasurable opportunities to learn, take care to not over-direct children's play as they need the time and space to create their own play. In outdoor settings particularly, there is a danger that the spaces are becoming institutionalised and over-sanitised (Waller 2007) and spontaneity needs to be allowed.

- Recalling our own experiences of childhood playing can increase our empathy with children. Focus particularly on the imaginative aspects of your play involving other worlds.

- In order to achieve balance in supporting children's play, adults need to provide children with the opportunities and spaces to engage in play, but also need to respect their abilities to create their own play spaces, particularly those which actively seek privacy from adults.

- For children there is often a distinct blurring of boundaries between the worlds of work and play, which they can slip in and out of effortlessly. Be mindful of the fact that the distinction is in fact an adult construction.

This chapter has provided a gentle introduction to the worlds in which children engage; worlds which can take them away from adults' eyes and adult direction; places where children can express themselves freely or become somebody else in another place or time. These worlds of play are, to a large extent, visible to adults through children's acting out of scenarios or through a trail of evidence left behind, of abandoned toys, treasure maps or the computer left on standby. Some of these worlds remain unseen as children create private play spaces in and out of which they weave, alongside undertaking their daily routines. However there are many more worlds to be discovered, which are even more hidden from adults' view.

CHAPTER 3

Seeing the unseen

Whilst play is often partially visible to the adult eye, some of the worlds which children inhabit are invisible to the adult eye. Children often 'see the unseen' – things which adults say do not exist and are simply figments of their imagination. Adults often do not even notice children's encounters with the unseen as they go about their hectic, daily business. This chapter takes a journey through these invisible worlds drawing on children's views and experiences, together with adults' recollections of their own in order to gain insight into how these phenomena are made manifest. A deeper exploration and discussion of the events from different academic perspectives follows later in chapter 6 and onwards, allowing this chapter to convey the worlds through the lens of childhood.

Recalling the hidden worlds of childhood reveals a range of memories, with regularly recurring themes of imaginary friends, seeing 'ghosts' or people who have died, or playing with fairies and elves. James remembers his childhood in the 1970s and the house he grew up in, in rural Devon in England. It was an old farmhouse with many outbuildings. He explained:

> The oldest part of the house was from the eighteenth century and I particularly loved being in a small, unused room upstairs which overlooked the field where our sheep grazed. I made the space my own, almost like a den, where I would play for hours. Often, an old man would come in and sit down in a shabby armchair and watch me. I used to talk to him but he didn't reply, just smiled at me, I never thought much about him because he was just someone who seemed to live in our house. But as I got older I wondered why my parents never mentioned

him and now I guess you might call him a ghost but at the time
I never thought twice about him being there.

In daily conversation, adults tend to refer to this aspect of children's
lives as being 'make-believe'. Children are often said to be using
their imagination and engaging in fantasy. For many adults, children
are simply playing games, perhaps making up ghost stories to scare
themselves or creating imaginary meals and drinks to share with
invisible friends. This chapter is deliberately unquestioning about the
experiences recounted in order to avoid seeing them through adult
lenses, instead hearing the children's voices, and adults' retrospective
childhood voices, as they describe their experiences. For now, the lens
of childhood takes prominence with the adult filters returning in the
later chapters to explore issues in a more critical and rigorous way.

Companions who cannot be seen

One of the most intriguing aspects of some children's lives is the
phenomenon of what are known as 'imaginary friends' in general
discourse. However, the term 'imaginary companions' is more
commonly applied in the academic literature (for example, by Taylor
1999, Hoff 2004, Kastenbaum and Fox 2007). It would appear that
imaginary companions have walked alongside children for many
years, with the first research into them being undertaken in 1895
by Vostrovosky (Singer and Singer 1990, Taylor 1999, Hoff 2004,
Kastenbaum and Fox 2007). Imaginary companions have also made
their way into literature including some works by Robert Louis
Stevenson, Mark Twain and Leo Tolstoy (Singer and Singer 1990).

In the late nineteenth century and early twentieth century there was
a strong belief that children who had imaginary companions had some
form of mental illness. As time progressed this view diminished and
new theoretical frameworks began to emerge, including psychoanalytic
approaches, some of which saw the child as having personality defects.
However many of these early studies have been criticised for relying on
children who were based in clinics and hospitals who were particularly
likely to have psychosocial problems (Taylor 1999, Hoff 2004). More
recent research has explored children's imaginary companions from a
variety of perspectives including aspects of children's developmental

progress, such as the relationship to children's creative potential and their ability to distinguish between fantasy and reality.

Researchers who study imaginary companions adopt a variety of approaches and definitions which has led to differing results. For example Singer and Singer (1990) include objects such as dolls and teddy bears if the children assign human qualities to them, whilst other researchers only include invisible companions. Such methodological differences naturally lead to various findings with regards to the frequency of the phenomenon although contemporary studies demonstrate that imaginary companions are relatively common. Singer and Singer (1990) interviewed 111 children and found that 65 per cent reported having one – a finding similar to Taylor (1999) who found a frequency of 63 per cent in her study of 100 children. In my discussions with 40 children, I used different terminology – that of 'invisible friends' – as I felt this was more appropriate to the children, some of whom were as young as four and may not have understood the phrase 'imaginary companions'. Sixteen (80%) said they thought that invisible friends were real, and a further two children were uncertain. Interestingly, the vast majority of these were in the upper age range of 8 to 11.

Darren, a businessman in his 40s, expressed a very common misconception when he said, 'Imaginary friends? No of course I didn't have one, why would I? I had my brothers to play with and I also had lots of friends so I didn't need to create any that didn't really exist. The only children who have them are those who are lonely.' Recent research has shown Darren's understanding to be incorrect; Taylor (1999) cites studies which show that children with imaginary companions were not shy and were in fact less fearful and anxious in their play than children who did not have them. Further, whilst there is some connection between the number of siblings and their place in the family it is not the case that the eldest or only children are those who have companions (Taylor 1999).

So, what are these companions like? Hallowell (2007) identifies four types. The most common, which he terms 'invizikids' (p. 29), are those who look and act conventionally according to their culture and historical era. They play with the children, and are usually good natured, occasionally having tantrums if they do not get their own way, and can select whether or not to disappear from the child's view when others enter the room. I spoke to Marianne, a social worker in her 50s, who vividly remembers her two companions from childhood who would fall into Hallowell's category of invizikids: a girl and a boy named Marjorie and Kicker who lived in the 'grey with black speckles gas oven' in the family's kitchen. Physically they were no different to other children. In fact Marianne recalled their appearances with intense clarity:

> Marjorie wore a yellow hand-knitted jumper and a red tartan skirt with a kilt pin. She wore pretty red patent leather shoes with a buckle. Her hair had a side parting and she wore a red bow in it. In contrast, Kicker – so called because he used to kick people – wore fawn socks with a green stripe and grey shorts. His knees were always dirty and full of scabs.

Marjorie and Kicker would open the oven door and creep out, and would often go out of the house with Marianne. In fact, Marianne recalls how she would refuse to cross the road unless they were by her side. Often they would linger behind, playing with each other, whilst Marianne's mother became increasingly impatient to get home. The two friends 'were as solid as you or I' she explained and remained in her life until the family moved house, when her mother said that they could not take the oven and it would be fairer to leave Marjorie and Kicker in their home.

In another example of a companion of this type, seven-year-old Caitlin (who was keen to inform me she was nearly eight), spoke enthusiastically about her invisible friend Poppy who had blonde hair. Caitlin first saw Poppy on her fifth birthday and was insistent that no one else could see her. I asked what she and Poppy did.

> 'We play together, we chat together and we eat together. Sometimes we eat outside in the garden. I make sure Mum and Dad give Poppy her invisible plate and things and sometimes I give her a drink. Sometimes when she is ill I look after her, like on Saturdays or Sundays and sometimes in the afternoon she comes to school with me. She has an invisible chair in the classroom.'

'So no one trips over her?' I asked.

'Yes, but they might walk through her,' Caitlin added.

Hallowell (2007) also found that some companions are animals who are gentle and caring. These include dogs, cats, snakes, lions, horses, frogs, budgerigars and mongooses and a particularly large number of elephants. He cites the story of Alan who recalled how his companion, a dog named Jugg, first appeared to him when he was three years old. Initially Jugg sat on a rug for five minutes staring at Alan before disappearing, but then gradually began to talk, building up to conversations. When Alan was eight years old, Jugg came to him in the garden and had a long conversation in which he explained that he wouldn't be able to see Alan again, and they said their goodbyes.

A smaller group of companions, according to Hallowell's (2007, p. 71) research are what he affectionately terms 'Wakkies'. These are divided into Sages who tend to be philosophical in nature and leave useless gifts, and Animates which are objects that become alive but only do so one, two or three times. He retells Jane's story of sitting in her living room near the hearth upon which sat a brush, shovel and a poker. One day the poker suddenly said 'hello' and a few days later he leapt from the hearth, having developed arms and legs. Mr Poker, as Jane called him, would talk to her, often reminding her of things she had forgotten but when Jane was ten years old, and after five or six visits, Mr Poker never became animated again. Finally, Hallowell (2007) also writes about the 'Elementals' – small creatures such as goblins and pixies who live outdoors, who will be considered later in this chapter.

These companions provide sources of comfort, enjoyment, amusement and friendship for the children who have them, but some can be sources of consternation, which are detailed in chapter 5 when exploring the darker sides of the unseen worlds. But for children, they are an integral and often unquestioned part of their life which can remain hidden from adults' view.

Seeing the deceased

In some cases, there may be a blurring of categories of 'unseen' beings. This is particularly evident when children report seeing people or animals which others cannot. These can be labelled imaginary companions, spirits of the deceased or ghosts depending on the context in which they are reported or experienced. The word 'ghost' is certainly in children's vocabulary, as they appear in books, both fiction and non-fiction, in films, television programmes, computer games and in tales told by older siblings and adults. Ghosts are represented as taking a variety of forms including the spirits of deceased people now dwelling in other realms, as friendly ghosts resembling white sheets who just want to have fun, or restless souls who are struggling to leave the place in which they lived and stay to haunt it. The latter, of which children can be fearful, will be discussed in chapter 5, but this section explores the ghosts that children see or sense who do not frighten them, which some people may term a 'spirit' of the deceased.

One of the most commonly reported phenomena of this type is the perceived presence of a person or pet who has died. Often children report these presences as a matter of course, initially unaware that adults or their peers remain oblivious to the presence. A good example is offered by a teacher called Ellen who recounted the tragic tale of the death of John, a ten-year-old pupil, in her school. John was killed in a car accident and Ellen and her colleagues worked hard to comfort the other children in the school when they broke the bad news to them. A few days later, several of the children began to tell Ellen that they had seen John playing in the school field. Far from being frightened by seeing him, the children were quite pragmatic about having seen him and did not question their experiences (Adams, Hyde and Woolley 2008). Nick, a 40-year-old Canadian, recalled an event which occurred when he was eleven years old. After dinner one evening, at precisely 7 p.m., he heard footsteps in what had originally been a passageway in a house prior to renovation. Nick asked who was there and his brother and sister-in-law replied, 'That's just Albert, he's caretaking.' Albert was Nick's deceased grandfather and his footsteps were often heard by the family, although this was the only occasion on which Nick had been aware of them. The encounter left Nick with feelings of safety and comfort.

Most experiences of children seeing the deceased involve them seeing, hearing or sensing people or pets who have been close to them, but on a small number of occasions the people are not personally known to them. I spoke to Saskia, aged ten, who had been an avid watcher of a television series presented by Steve Irwin, an Australian wildlife expert who became known as the crocodile hunter. Irwin was famous for his conservation work, particularly with dangerous animals and in 2006 was tragically killed in the course of his work, by a fatal piercing by a stingray in the Australian Great Barrier Reef. Saskia explained that:

> He [Steve Irwin] is like, there, lots of the time. I saw him this morning sort of in the playground but a bit up in the trees so he wasn't standing on the ground. Well I saw his face, not his whole body. He was just smiling, looking at a bird that was on a branch. Then sometimes I think he has disappeared but I see him again.

Saskia was more intrigued by what she saw than frightened by it and could not offer an explanation.

Marianne, who enjoyed life with her two invisible friends Marjorie and Kicker, also recalled seeing an elderly lady in the second house into which her family moved. The house was already furnished when the family moved in and a rocking chair was positioned near the fire in the living room. Marianne's mother would regularly move it away from the fire, telling her daughter that it was dangerous to have it so close. But Marianne would constantly push it back, explaining that 'the old lady likes sitting there'. Marianne and the old lady never spoke to each other, but the child was concerned that the lady should be kept warm. Later, Marianne was to learn that an elderly lady who had since died had previously lived in the house. In a similar story, Hart (2003) retells the account of a young girl named Sydney, aged 18 months, who lived in an old American house. Her parents recalled how Sydney would spend time staring at a rocking chair, seemingly looking at it as if it were moving backwards and forwards. Sometimes she would point to it and say 'lady!' Her parents distinctly remembered the time when Sydney saw some photographs that lay in a desk in the house. She pointed to one, which pictured a woman, and she exclaimed 'lady!' When asked if it was the same lady whom Sydney saw in her room, she replied 'yupeeee!!' The photograph was of Sydney's great grandmother who lived in the house 20 years before Sydney was born (Hart 2003, p.133; Adams et al. 2008, p. 30). Such reports of children apparently seeing people who have died are very common and often cause no distress to the children, who simply assume that others see what they see.

Fairies

Fairies, elves and nature spirits have a very long history in the traditions of many countries and are also the topic of many children's stories in Western countries. Indeed, in Europe, fairy tales have been read to millions of children over time, telling them of the little people who live in the woodlands. Pictures often show them as tiny human-like figures, some with wings, making their homes near toadstools and drinking from cups made from acorns.

Carrie, a five-year-old girl, described in careful detail the fairies which she regularly sees in her garden. 'I just about seen her because she was just very like the plant [pink in colour] and she was very tiny. On a different flower I saw a red fairy because it was like a poppy.' I asked what happened when she saw them. Carrie explained that they didn't see her as they were taking things to make honey, moving from flower to flower. As they landed on a new one, they turned into the same colour as the new flower, as a chameleon might. This was in order to avoid being seen. I asked why this was and Carrie explained: 'Because sometimes they have little private things and sometimes people are dangerous because people might stand on them.' Her classmate Finn, also aged five, interrupted to say, 'Pretend you are tiny and someone comes running to you, you would be scared.'

I was intrigued to know if other members of her family had also seen the garden fairies. Carrie often told her mum, dad and brother that they were there but she said:

> The fairies just fly away because they think, they hear them, and they think they're going to stand on them, so now I learned that, so I tell my family to whisper and be very quiet so they can see them but they never do because they can't get there in time.

The fairies can also hang in the air, without moving, 'like dragonflies,' Carrie continued. This is another strategy to avoid being seen by humans, 'so no one can touch them… because they think people will pick them up and throw them,' Finn added.

Phoebe and Oliver, aged nine, told of their encounters with the little people. Pheobe explained about the fairy she saw in her house.

I seen one in my bedroom before. It was a tiny sparkle – my whole bedroom was really dark, kind of a sparkle and it started dancing about. It was a tiny, tiny creature and it had a bright green dress on, yellow, like a gold glow around it. For some reason it didn't have a wand though.

'Not all fairies have to carry a wand,' Oliver interjected and then continued with his own story. 'I saw a little elf before... in my bedroom, under my bed... he was small and had a hat. He was dancing, he was green.'

For all of these children, the experiences seemed very normal and they were able to justify their encounters when asked. A continuing theme which emerged in our discussions on this topic was the tooth fairy, whom most children believed in and some had seen. The tooth fairy will reappear in chapter 7 because she represents an interesting paradox in understanding adults' responses to children's experiences of the unseen.

Journeys into other worlds? Near-death experiences

The worlds described above tend to be regular elements of some children's lives, which are familiar to people because they are a major part of many cultures. A more unusual experience, which happens only to a very small minority of people, and usually as a one-off event, is a near-death experience (NDE). Kellehear (1996, p. 4) describes the popular image of an NDE as consisting of a person being seriously ill or involved in an accident when their heart stops beating and resuscitation begins. After revival, they tell a story involving a feeling of great peace, undertaking a review of their own life, an out-of-body experience, a sensation of moving through a tunnel, and encountering bright lights and/or deceased relatives or friends. Greyson (2006) also notes that these experiences can involve a sensing or seeing of mystical figures or presences and feelings of oneness or sacredness and transcendence of time. Prior to the NDE there is no direct correlation with a religious belief although afterwards many people report new religious affiliations or spiritual awareness, often re-evaluating their lives.

During an NDE, people often report seeing or being in another world. Whilst NDEs are generally associated with adults, children have also reported them. Melvin Morse (Morse and Perry 1990, Morse 2001) and his colleagues conducted a controlled clinical study of children's NDEs at Seattle Children's Hospital, USA. Morse commented that these children were too young to know what an NDE was, yet they recounted very similar stories to those of adults though usually without undertaking a life review. Other authors such as Greyson (2006) have, however, suggested some additional differences such as tending not to meet deceased friends or family although some accounts from children in Morse and Perry's study (1990) suggest otherwise. The International Association for Near-Death Studies (2006) states that children's NDEs also differ in that they are more likely to include a visitation by a deceased pet or other animal, relatives whom they do not know and occasionally by people who are still alive.

Morse and Perry (1990) concluded from their study of 12 children that each had experiences of at least one of the following: an out-of-body experience; a tunnel; seeing people who had died; seeing a being of light; a life review; a conscious desire to return to their body; and seeing light. The last is a recurring theme.

The following are examples of accounts of adults' recollections of childhood NDEs, drawn from North America and the UK, in their own words. Hart (2003) retells the story of Robert, an American psychologist, who was in a car crash when he was 11 years old. His leg was crushed in between the car and the brick wall it had collided with and he was rushed to hospital for surgery. Complications followed the operation and he began to slowly bleed to death. He remembered a strong determination not to die when suddenly he 'crossed a divide' and found himself in a world of 'pure light, gold, radiant, luminous, ecstatically happy, perfectly beautiful, purely tranquil, joy beyond bound...' Robert continued,

> I wasn't the least bit interested in anything on the earthly side of the divide; I could only revel at what was before me... It was all that any mystic ever promised of heaven, and I knew then that I was in possession of the greatest treasure known to humankind.
>
> (Hart 2003, p. 220)

Despite, or perhaps because of, this epiphany, Robert found it difficult to return to earthly life, struggling to find meaning and purpose that could compare with what he had seen of this other world.

A feeling of being saved was prominent in the narrative of Penny, a Canadian woman, who had a near-death experience when she was six years old after almost drowning in a motel swimming pool. She reported her experience to Scott (2004). As she lay in the water she mentally began to say goodbye to people and prayed. She saw an old man sitting at the side of the pool who was not physically there. As she then said goodbye to her cousin, to whom she was very close, she suddenly felt that she was not ready to die. Somebody saved her at that moment. She felt many emotions and sensations including fear, a warm glowing light, anger at God's lack of presence, sadness and happiness. Afterwards she described how powerful the NDE had been in showing her that there was a greater being protecting her and that life continued after the physical one.

Moody (2001, p. 21) observes how people often report a noise accompanied by a sensation of being pulled quickly through a dark space such as a tunnel, cave, valley or void. He narrates the account of a 36-year-old man who had a near-death experience when he was nine years old. The boy had been rushed to hospital where doctors gave him ether and his heart stopped beating. He explained:

> I heard this ringing noise, brrrrnnnng–brrrrnnnng–brrrrnnnng, very rhythmic. Then I moved through this – you're going to think this is weird – through this long dark place. It seems like a sewer or something. I just can't describe it to you. I was moving, beating all the time with this noise, this ringing noise.

The theme of moving through a tunnel is not untypical of NDEs and is also featured in Ann's narrative, as reported by Atwater (2004). Ann, an American woman, had an NDE when she was ten years old after being electrocuted by a 220 volt wire which she grabbed onto to stop herself falling off a swing. She explained:

> I remember my spirit leaving my body through my head and travelling straight upward to an open tunnel, which was dark but not scary. I was travelling at a very fast speed and after a

while the tunnel became transparent. I saw specks of twinkling light and other spirits travelling in tunnels parallel to mine, some upward and some downward. Next I reached the end of my tunnel and began to free float in one spot in space.

Whilst floating, Ann saw her recently deceased grandmother who spoke to her telepathically to tell her it was her time to go back. Ahead was a huge cloud of light from which a voice said that the choice was hers. Ann continued:

I was perfectly happy to just stay there for all eternity, but my grandmother's comment had made me realise that there was more that needed to be accomplished in my life. At that instant, I was swooped away back down the tunnel and soon hovered above my ten-year-old body. I thought, how could I ever fit into that tiny body? Finally, I remember waking up with my father leaning over me and my family staring at me.

Near-death experiences thus often appear to give recipients glimpses into what they describe as a world beyond this one: an afterlife. For those who had encountered them, these are no *imaginary* worlds. They are very real worlds which can significantly affect their outlook and philosophy on life. Morse and Perry (1990) revisited the children they had interviewed when they were older to research any potential impact the NDE had on their lives in the long term and found that whilst for a small number it was simply something which had happened, for others transformation was a key feature. Tom, who had almost drowned at the age of five, later explained to Morse that the experience had been responsible for him 'sorting out his life' by leaving him with an urgent desire to acquire knowledge. He became interested in science and engineering to help him discover 'the natural order of things', and by his 40s had gained an international reputation in science (p.145).

Occasionally the doors to other worlds remain open after revival as Denise, an American who had an NDE after collapsing into a diabetic coma and suffering from a stroke when she was ten years old, found. She subsequently told her father that since her coma she had been able to see auras around people as well as the spirits of people who had died (Atwater 2004).

Religious worlds

For some children, worlds which they encounter – or the figures they meet there – can be described as explicitly religious by the experients and/or the commentators. These can take different forms as the following section illustrates, such as seeing religious figures whilst awake, in dreams or in near-death experiences. These experiences are by no means intended to be exhaustive, for they can take many different forms, but the three categories included here are used to demonstrate the variety of encounters which research suggests occur in childhood.

ANGELS

Many children readily identify with the concept of angels which is unsurprising given that they are found in different religions and cultures throughout the world as well as having become a popular theme in the 'New Age' movement in the West where they are often presented as 'guardian angels' who protect humans. Images of angels are readily available, with renowned artists including Michelangelo, Botticelli and Raphael having depicted them, alongside images created by children's authors and illustrators to be found in books, films, television programmes and other digital media.

In my own research with 40 children aged 4–11, over half of the children believed in them (n=25) with a further four 'half' believing in them. The children's reasons for asserting their existence were often grounded in what children deemed to be evidence, such as 'they're true because they are in the Bible'. But do children experience angelic presences? Research suggests that some do, and not surprisingly, their descriptions of angels often match their conscious image of them. Hart (2003, p. 2) claims that many children report seeing angels, which often come in the form of a guardian angel watching over them. He describes one case in particular, that of his daughter Haley, aged six, who was settling down to sleep one evening. Hart was saying good night when she said that she felt a little light-headed, a feeling that she had experienced before. She explained that after this sensation she often saw her angels and commented, 'Yeah, I do see them and it's like I can feel them and know they're there. It's like they're having a tea party and they're talking about me.' Far from being frightened, Haley felt very comforted by their presence, finishing her conversation with the words, 'they let me know I'm loved' as she drifted off to sleep.

Similar accounts of being unafraid in angelic presences are to be found in the work of Newcomb (2008), a writer for the general audience, who has collected people's experiences of angels over many years. Amongst her reports are several cases of young children seeing one. One mother asked her five-year-old daughter if she had ever seen an angel, and was surprised when she recounted a trip to a zoo the year before. Whilst looking at rabbits, her daughter saw an angel of a similar age to herself with blonde hair and wings. The angel remained by her side for some time before she flew in the air and circled behind her. The mother remembered the occasion, having noticed that her daughter was watching something. This was the first of several occasions when the young girl reported similar incidents. Newcomb (2008) also spoke to Vicky, a woman who remembered an incident from childhood when she and her sister were awoken by the sound of tapping on the window. She got out of bed to investigate but could not see anything out of her bedroom window so she sneaked into her brothers' room. The tapping appeared to be coming from their window and as Vicky drew back the curtains she was stunned to see seven angels in the garden who told her she was very special. Vicky was confused that she could hear the angels clearly even though they were outside the house, and she rushed to her parents' room. Her mother came to look but could see nothing, despite the fact that Vicky could still see them waving to her. The scent of flowers suddenly filled the room which even her mother could smell. She asked her daughter if she had been spraying perfume, an accusation which she denied (Newcomb 2008).

Jonas, a seven-year-old boy, to whom I spoke, used the terminology 'fairy' and 'angel' interchangeably as he described his encounter with a winged being when he was five years old. He explained that 'it was pretty big'. He was with his cousin who was 16 and they were in a park one evening. 'She had white wings and silver shoes on, silky shoes, and she... um... as soon as we saw her she went straight back up to heaven. It was there for like half an hour.' Apparently she spoke in a very gentle voice although he could not remember what she had said as he had 'only been five'.

Seeing or sensing the presence of religious and/or spiritual figures does not occur only whilst awake, as it did for the above-mentioned children, but can also happen during sleep. Dreams can often be a vehicle for children (and adults) to enter other worlds, and are the focus of the following chapter. For some children and teenagers, dreams are places in which they encounter angels, as Samantha, a ten-year-old Scottish girl, described to me. Samantha had a pet hamster named Hammy who had been ill. Naturally, she was particularly upset, but had a dream in which an angel appeared and said 'Hammy would be happier and he would be looked after well and he wouldn't feel any pain or anything.' Samantha took comfort in the angel's words; whilst realising that Hammy was likely to die in the near future, she also was reassured that Hammy would have a happy life after his physical death. Her independent interpretation of the dream was that the angel had told her about his forthcoming death 'in a nice way' and the dream not only helped her to come to terms with the impending loss but also gave her the encouragement to support her younger siblings. For Samantha, the angel was real and restored her confidence in the belief in an afterlife (Adams and Hyde 2008).

OTHER RELIGIOUS FIGURES
Angels are not the only religious/spiritual figures which can appear in young people's dreams, as Siegel and Bulkeley's (1998) description of Ted's significant dream illustrates. Ted was brought up in a Protestant family in the USA but they had not encouraged him to be involved in religion and Ted's own belief was that there were many ways to find true spirituality, not just through Christianity. When he was 16 he had a dream in which Jesus came to him and said that, 'no one could get to the Father but through him' (p. 169). Ted believed that this was a message indicating that Christianity was the way forward for him and it influenced his major life decision, some years later, to join a seminary.

Although less common than waking encounters or dreams, but equally fascinating, are children's encounters with religious figures during near-death experiences. Morse and Perry's (1990) study includes several accounts of children seeing or meeting religious figures including God, Jesus and angels. One nine-year-old girl, Katie, was in intensive care after a swimming pool accident in a hospital in Idaho, USA, and was resuscitated by Doctor Morse. When he later asked her what she remembered about being in the swimming pool she explained that she 'met Jesus and the Heavenly Father' together with Elizabeth who appeared in a tunnel. Elizabeth was an angel who was tall with bright golden hair. Morse was intrigued and discussed the family's religious beliefs with Katie's parents and discovered that the family did not believe in guardian angels or tunnels to heaven.

In another account given to Morse, 43-year-old Kathleen recalled her accident as a nine year old when walking on a log in shallow water. She slipped off it into the river and the log fell on top of her, holding her head under water. Although the water was very cold, she felt warm and found herself under a blue, cloudless sky with a large fluffy circle glowing in it. A hand reached out of the circle to draw her into the next world but Kathleen did not want to go and withdrew her hand. Kathleen sensed that there was a God in the light, but not the God perceived by the several religions with which she had been involved in later life and she concluded that she did not need formalised religion to be with God.

Children's descriptions of seeing, hearing or sensing the presence of transcendental figures can take various forms and whilst they are often associated with an individual's religious upbringing, they are also reported by children with no faith background. It is thus important to begin to consider the impact of the wider culture upon children's experiences of unseen worlds so that adults can achieve a wider understanding of them.

PREVIOUS LIVES IN *THIS* WORLD

Whilst the worlds discussed thus far pertain to children weaving in and out of realms on a daily basis, but very much being in the present, some children appear to recall having lived in this world before, prior to their current existence. The notion of reincarnation is not inherent in traditional Western philosophies, although the concept has become increasingly popular amongst many exploring alternative or New Age philosophies. Stevenson (1987) has studied over 2000 accounts of reincarnation throughout the world and has paid particular attention to cases in which children appear to remember previous lives. One such example he details is that of Samuel, a Finnish boy, who made many statements indicating that he was not Samuel, but Pertti who was his uncle who had died one year prior to Samuel's birth. At the age of one-and-a-half, Samuel began telling people that his name was Pertti, which he continued to do until he was six years old. When looking at photographs of his uncle, Samuel would often say 'that's me' (p.74). One day, whilst looking at a photograph of Pertti, Samuel explained how he had been bitten by a dog. That had never happened to him, but had happened to Pertti when he was three years old. Samuel had never been told about this incident and nothing in the photograph suggested having being bitten. Samuel also called his parents by their first names – but instead of using their own names, he used those of his grandparents who were, of course, Pertti's parents. Bowman (1998) also explores children's accounts and includes one of a two-year-old girl, Liaa, who unexpectedly shouted out 'This is where I died!' as her mother was driving. Her mother stopped the car and asked what Liaa meant and she explained that she had been in a car without wearing her seatbelt when the car had driven off a bridge and plunged into water below. Liaa told how she had felt the sensation of rocks falling on her head before she drowned. Her parents reported that Liaa would continue to relate this story for the next year and a half, without ever deviating from the original version.

Such accounts are quite typical of those reported, which tend to show that young children such as these talk in quite matter-of-fact ways about having lived before. Some cases, such as Samuel's, resonate with the family's history, whilst in others, the cases appear to relate to completely separate situations not known to the family. Although to some extent these children are talking about having lived in this world, they can perhaps be said to have one foot in a world which has been extremely real to them. As with all the topics covered in this book, readers are invited to draw their own conclusions as to the 'reality' of children's reports. Those who are interested in pursuing this topic of children who appear to claim to having previously lived before are referred to the various books by Ian Stevenson.

OTHER TERRITORIES

Many of the phenomena detailed above, with the notable exception of
near-death experiences and perhaps past-life memories, are reasonably
regular occurrences of childhood and fall neatly into the categories
laid out. However, not all experiences are so easily classified and it
is important to be aware of those which do not sit comfortably in a
socially recognised type. One such example was presented to me by
Matt, an American teacher in his 40s, who vividly remembered the
time he literally saw another world when he was nine years old. He
said,

> It was late spring and there were beautiful cloud formations.
> The sun was low and the clouds looked red. I was gazing and I
> saw a whole city in the clouds. It looked like Jerusalem – there
> were houses in the hillside…

Matt explained that this was not a simple case of seeing pictures in the
clouds. Instead, this was an incredibly intricate image which looked
like a drawing rather than a photograph. It was a 'profound' moment
and his story continues in chapter 9. Matt's narrative is one example
of experiences of other worlds which does not fit into an easily
recognisable category, and undoubtedly others will also exist which
have not been covered here. Examples such as Matt's demonstrate the
importance of not only being open-minded about possibilities but
also to be aware that children may experience something which is not
in our own immediate consciousness.

Empathising with children who see the unseen

It is possible that of all the aspects of children's unseen worlds
detailed in this book, it is those in this chapter that will be the most
challenging for some readers to empathise with. Chapter 7 will look
more closely at the reasons why it can be difficult for adults to fully
understand these aspects of children's lives, but for now it is worth
trying to recall our experiences of what others around us did not see.
Inevitably, the range of experiences will be vast and may include those
detailed in this chapter and/or additional ones. Conversely, it may be
that some readers cannot recall any such events, but if experiences
can be remembered it is important to try to recall the feelings that

accompanied them. In some cases, the experiences will have created a strong impression which has lasted into adulthood, but for many, like James in his farmhouse, there may have been no particularly strong responses at the time. This is particularly likely to be the case when the child assumes that what they see or hear is 'normal', often only later discovering that others did not or do not experience similar things. Ultimately, adults need to attempt to understand the child's experience as the child is reporting it and even if this proves too difficult, perhaps because it is counter-intuitive, practitioners should be prepared to offer a sympathetic and interested ear.

Some recommendations

- Be alert to the possibility of children's encounters with the unseen. The range is wide and the topics covered in this book are by no means intended to be an exhaustive list.

- Retain an open mind. You may regard invisible companions as a form of imaginary/fantasy play but for some children there is a strong likelihood that these companions are very real. Other children may well describe these companions as friends which they have 'made up' in order to pass the time with them, but it is important that you do not jump to conclusions. You can only know for certain what the child's beliefs are if you ask them.

- Do not assume that a child with a particularly unusual account such as a near-death experience has been significantly affected by it; some will have simply accepted it as something which has happened. If adults assume or infer that there is something special or profound about the experience, it could lead to a child embellishing their report in order to gain attention.

- Take care to avoid stereotyping about children's experiences, particularly religious ones, based on their backgrounds. Children of no faith report encounters with figures which may be deemed religious. Children are exposed to religious language and art in everyday life and these images and ideas can be assimilated into their consciousness even if they are not from religious homes.

- When using material such as books or multi-media which deal with topics such as fairies, imaginary companions or ghosts in a fictional manner, be aware that whilst children will recognise that the story in hand is fantasy, they may simultaneously believe that the beings can exist. Further, this way of thinking is not always confined to the younger children. For example, in my study of unseen worlds, 95 per cent of the children aged 8–11 (n=19) believed that ghosts were real compared to 25 per cent (n=5) of the children aged 4–7. Although such statistics will vary from group to group, they serve to warn that making assumptions about what children believe to be real or fictional, based on their age and maturity, can be unwise.

- Even if you do not believe in the possibility of seeing the unseen, many children are able to justify their ability to do so articulately, sometimes defending them against alternative explanations. When nine-year-olds, Phoebe and Oliver, were sharing their respective experiences of seeing a fairy and an elf, they were sat in a group with an older classmate, Huw, who remained a little sceptical. Respectfully, Huw suggested that his friends might have been uncertain as to whether they had been awake or dreaming. Phoebe replied 'I know I was awake cos I pinched myself and it hurt!' When probed further, she added that the fairy was floating and 'people can't do that'.

This chapter has touched on the worlds of dreams, which children enter on a nightly basis. Research indicates that many people report one or two dreams which have significantly impacted on them, often having occurred during childhood. The following chapter leaves the experiences of daylight and wakefulness and enters the darkness of the night to begin to explore the unseen worlds which children enter after the sun has set.

CHAPTER 4

The worlds at night

The worlds which children inhabit are not restricted to those in waking hours. Each night as children sleep, they enter new worlds in which anything can happen. This is the world of dreaming in which children can fly, battle monsters, be a superhero, travel to other planets or simply talk with friends. Throughout the world, throughout history, dreams have captured the imagination of people. Records from ancient civilisations show that dreams were often considered to be messages from the gods. This belief was so strong that many civilisations built dream incubation temples where a person in need of an answer to a question would perform rituals before sleeping there, invoking the gods into their dreams to provide a solution (Van de Castle 1994, Adams 2003). Our ancestors also observed that some dreams appear to predict the future, informing humans of what is to come, whether it be of minor happenings or world disasters.

The exploration of dreams has taken an interesting journey across different cultures and different eras, being associated with gods and demons, as journeys of the soul taking leave of the body at night, as phenomena investigated in the sleep laboratory and as insights from the subconscious mind. But whatever perspective a person chooses to take when attempting to explain their dreams, over a lifetime they will encounter a range of different types. Some will give pleasure and reassurance; others will arouse curiosity and evoke strong emotions; some will leave anxiety or fear; and a small number will make a significant impact upon the dreamer and their impression will remain with them throughout their life.

This chapter explores these worlds which children inhabit during sleep. After a focus on the dreams which adults recall from their own youth, a brief background to the developments in scientific research follows, before a deeper exploration of children's accounts is made in order to gain insights to these nightly journeys. Using the children's own words where possible, the impact of significant dreams is conveyed, showing how they can influence their waking thoughts and behaviour.

Remembering childhood dreams

Can you remember any dreams from childhood? Researchers have indicated that the majority of adults' recollections of their earliest dream is of one from childhood. For example, Fiske and Pillemer (2006) conducted two studies with 96 Caucasian and 79 Asian women aged 17–22 in the USA, in which they were given a questionnaire and asked to recall their earliest dream. Overall they found that participants were able to remember dreams from a very young age, though rarely from before the age of three.

Similarly, Bulkeley *et al.* (2005) asked 109 adults living in the northwest of the USA if they could recall their earliest remembered dream. Eighty-five were able to do so, and recalled a dream which they had had between the ages of 3 and 12. When the researchers analysed the nature of the dream reports, they noted that many had a particularly vivid intensity to them; frightening nightmares were common, whilst a quarter of the dreams were positive in nature, such as fulfilling a wish, encountering a spiritual being and being able to fly. The intensity of the dreams reported by Bulkeley's team is understandable, as events which impact upon us are more likely to remain in the memory, in part because of their emotional strength and in part because of the tendency to rehearse the memory, thereby reinforcing it.

Nightmares are common in childhood (Woolley and Wellman 1992, Hartmann 1996, Siegel and Bulkeley 1998), as the following chapter details, so it naturally follows that for many people their earliest recollection of a dream is in fact of a nightmare. Abhik, now in his 30s, vividly remembers a recurring childhood nightmare in which he was chased around his house by a shadowy figure. He would run and run, becoming breathless, circling the house with the figure close behind him until he awoke in a cold sweat shouting for help. However, other memorable childhood dreams are less threatening and can be spiritually meaningful (Siegel and Bulkeley 1998, Adams 2003). Siegel and Bulkeley (1998) note that this type of dream may or may not have religious imagery and is distinguished by their felt power. They describe Peter's dream as an example. Peter recalled the dream he had when he was seven years old, over 40 years ago, in which he saw a burning angel inside his house near the front door. Everything was on fire and the house and the angel were falling apart in the midst of hot glowing flames. To the listener this dream may sound like a nightmare but Peter did not feel any fear. Instead he was amazed by the brightness and vibrancy of the flames and he believed that the dream was telling him something important about the world. It was like he had glimpsed into intense life energies which were radiant but destructive at the same time. He explained, 'after the dream, I always had this special confidence inside me that I knew about the secret of the fire; even if no one else could see it, I always knew it was there, very close to me' (p.163).

These two examples of Abhik and Peters' memories illustrate how nightmares can remain with a person for a lifetime – and a theme expanded upon below. Of course, not all dreams are memorable either in childhood or adulthood, and it is the minority that make an impact on individuals. However, that impact can be a significant one, but before I focus on those dream worlds, I offer a brief overview of what researchers from different disciplines have discovered about children's dreams through the decades in order to contextualise the discussion of the places to which children travel in their dreams.

An overview of children's dream worlds

In the 1950s, scientists working in US sleep laboratories identified that the period of sleep known as rapid eye movement (REM) sleep was accompanied by particularly vivid dreaming. For decades this type of sleep was assumed to be synonymous with dreaming, although more recent studies have shown that people also dream in the non-REM sleep state. However, studies into REM sleep have uncovered interesting findings when comparing adults' sleep to that of children, showing that the amount of REM sleep decreases as people get older. Flanagan (2000) reports that newborn babies spend approximately 50 per cent of their sleep in REM, which drops to 33 per cent at the age of three months. This amount continues to decrease further into adulthood, with adults spending approximately 20 per cent of their sleep in the REM state (Mallon 1989, Garfield 2001). For children then, dreaming occupies a considerable period of their lives. If children spend so much time dreaming, of what do they dream and how do the dreams affect them? This section begins with an overview of the typical dream content that children report before moving on to offer examples of dreams which have been particularly significant.

DREAMS OF EVERYDAY LIFE, PEOPLE AND PLACES

The majority of dreams naturally reflect our daily lives – the people we know, the places we go to, the images we see and the things we think about, from both our present and our past. Quantitative studies have analysed dream content by their components, which include settings and characters. Strauch and Lederbogen (1999) analysed the content of 299 dreams of children aged 9–15 in a longitudinal study, and examined the settings of their dreams. They observe that the settings in the children's dreams are primarily outdoors and contain an equal combination of familiar and unfamiliar places, remaining constant throughout the duration of the study. Resnick et al. (1994) also studied settings in the dreams of four- to ten-year-olds. They identify school as the most frequent setting, followed by home and vehicles. Home settings were more frequent in the dreams of eight- to ten-year-olds than in those of four- to five-year-olds, when school settings were more common, possibly because school was a new experience for them and occupied their waking thoughts for more time.

Dream characters have also been scrutinised. Resnick et al. (1994) report that the four- to ten-year-olds in their study most frequently cited family members as the characters in their dreams, which totalled 30 per cent of all characters. Similarly, in Punamäki's (1999) work exploring the dream content of 413 children aged 6–15, family members appeared more frequently in girls' dreams than boys', and older children dreamt more of peers than the younger children did. Such quantitative studies thus suggest that the worlds of children's dreams are predominantly related to their daily lives, filled with home, school, friends and family. But other worlds also intrude.

For many children in the West, television occupies a considerable part of their lives. Gunter and McAleer (1997) note the difficulties which are inherent in methodologies that seek to establish how much television children watch, but state that studies generally show that consistent television viewing tends to begin at the age of two. With increased accessibility to all forms of media in the lives of Western children (at home, at school, visits to the cinema, and/or at friends' homes for example), children are exposed to more visual and auditory phenomena than ever before in history. It is thus unsurprising to learn that the images from television and computer games often weave their way into children's dreams. An American boy aged five told of how he dreamt he was at the beach with his brother and mother, where Wishbone – a talking dog from a US television programme – had been taken prisoner on an island. The boy went to the island with two puppet characters from a different show and together they fought the guards in order to rescue Wishbone (Siegel and Bulkeley 1998).

The content of much of our dreams is obviously derived from daily activities and thoughts – something which Freud (1900/1999) termed day residue – and hence many are often instantly forgotten. Dreams are not just reflections of the present but also incorporate memories as well, and whether a dream is predominantly present- or past-focused, the experience of it can still be quite intense. Yet not all dreams are so easy to explain and some hold particular fascination and make significant impact on the individual.

Seeing the future

Amidst the mundane content of most dreams, lie specific types of dreams which capture the imagination and sometimes appear to defy explanation. One such phenomenon which is regularly reported in studies of children's dreams is that of precognitive dreams: dreams which appear to predict the future. There is of course a wealth of difficulties in verifying reports of dreams that are claimed to foretell future events. The primary difficulty relates to the reliability of the data because the dreamer cannot always verify that either they had the dream and/or that the alleged foreseen event subsequently took place. If, for example, the individual reports both the dream and its event in retrospect, the researcher may have no means of proving that their claims are authentic. The researcher needs to ask questions such as 'did they dream it before the event? Did they have the dream at all? Did the event subsequently occur? How closely did the dream's content match the event?' That said, what is important to acknowledge is that if children attach meaning to a dream because they believe it has predicted the future, then their assignation of meaning gives it personal significance irrespective of the objective scientific evidence which may or may not be available.

Despite these complications, adults in a variety of studies have reported having precognitive dreams during childhood. Fukuda (2002) surveyed 122 university students in Japan about their experiences of precognitive dreams. Forty-one people (33.6%) reported them, and the majority asserted that they began encountering them between the ages of six and ten.

Mallon (2002) also suggests that precognitive dreams are a common feature of children's experiences and cites a girl who described how she regularly had dreams about minor events about her family which later occurred. In my own interviews with children, a ten-year-old girl named Georgina explained that most of her dreams predicted the future. These were invariably about small events that took place in the course of her daily routine:

> Just things like we're doing in maths in school and spelling and I'm getting words wrong. And then it happens two days later but it only happens in about two days if it's going to happen at all.
>
> Georgina

Dreams of the future can have different impacts upon children. Some, such as Georgina, thought little of them because they were so common for her. For others, even if the content is unsettling, such dreams can provide reassurance. Ahmed, a British Muslim boy, described his dream to me.

> I was on my bike going down the hill and the bike was going really fast. Then suddenly straight ahead of me was a tree. I was going to crash into it but then I swerved and just missed it! And the next day it really happened.
>
> Ahmed

Ahmed explained that the following day he was on his bike and found himself in the same situation that the dream portrayed. As he approached the tree he recalled the dream and steered away from it, with no injury sustained. Ahmed's response to the dream was a calm one. He perceived it to be a warning of a possible accident – a warning which had alerted him to the possibility so that he could take evasive action. When I asked about the origin of the warning he said, 'The dream came from Allah. Only Allah knows the future.' For Ahmed, the dream was a sign that Allah was protecting and guiding him and hence the dream offered him reassurance and security.

Naturally, some children may have had a different response to a dream like Ahmed's, possibly fearing that any dream which conveyed an unpleasant scenario may actually occur and children's concerns over dreams and nightmares are considered in the following chapter.

Dreams of heaven

Angels and heaven are common features of dreams for children and have been for many decades. In the 1930s, Kimmins (1931) conducted the earliest large-scale study of 4861 dreams of subjects aged from 5 to 18. He asked the children and young people to recount their most recent dream, and found that girls aged 12–13 regularly dreamt of religion in general and heaven in particular, although he did not provide any specific information about the frequency of them or their content.

This theme has continued into contemporary society. Mallon's (1989) study includes a sample of children living in sectarian Northern Ireland and she observes that many of their dreams had religious content that reflected their religious upbringing. Adrian, a 12-year-old boy, dreamt of being in heaven with his deceased relatives, all floating on a bubble of sugar. In her later study, Mallon (2002) cites three examples of angels appearing in dreams, one of which was of a 12-year-old girl who regularly dreamt that an angel sat at the end of her bed guarding her throughout the night. In another, a 13-year-old boy described how he had been ill when he was five years old and at the time had dreamt that an angel entered his room to talk to his mother, who explained that her son was ill. The angel blessed him and, in the dream, his illness was instantly cured.

In my own study in England of 66 children aged 9–11 from both Christian and secular backgrounds, a fifth reported having dreamt about God at some point in their lives. These dreams included Bridie's in which she travelled to heaven which had 'big gold gates and there was just loads and loads of little bits with beds in,' and a shop selling 'spirit candy' – sweets for spirits to buy when they go to heaven (Adams 2001, p. 104). Ann explained how she had had an argument with her friend at school which had upset her. In the dream God appeared and gave her some advice on how to resolve the problems with her friend.

This category of dreams is important for practitioners to acknowledge because it is easy to assume that if children are not from religious homes that they will not experience religious dreams. This is not necessarily the case. Some children such as Ann will understand them as a means of solving problems. Others will believe them to be encounters with the divine, even if they are not from faith backgrounds. Others will believe themselves reunited in heaven with deceased pets and relatives or take comfort in 'seeing' that heaven exists.

The 'big dreams' of childhood

Some of the dreams cited above, particularly those in the precognitive category, may also be of particular significance to children because they can stand out from the majority of the dreams which they experience. Whilst there may, then, be some overlap in this section, I now move on to explore what the eminent psychoanalyst Carl Jung referred to as 'big' dreams. These, he said, were the 'richest jewel in the treasure house of psychic experience' (Jung 1948, p. 290). Some appear to have special qualities – ones which are not easy to define or articulate, and are often ethereal in nature. Whilst such dreams do not occur regularly, when they do they can bring with them instinctive feelings of significance, alongside strong emotions and may remain in our memory for the rest of our life. Jung identified different periods of time during one's life when such dreams are likely to occur, one of which was during childhood. Whatever their content, the essential, and defining, quality of a big dream is that it leaves a feeling of significance in the dreamer (Adams 2003).

When exploring children's big dreams it is important for adults to acknowledge that what is significant for one person may not be significant for another. It is essential that the adult listens carefully to what the child is saying about their dream. It may indeed seem inconsequential to the adult ear but could be particularly meaningful for the child. Research indicates, as the examples below illustrate, that many children find meaning in some of their dreams. Whilst it is not the practitioner's place to suggest that dreams have meaning, or to 'interpret' dreams in settings such as schools, care centres or nurseries, children's reflections upon their dreams can provide fascinating insights into how they perceive their dream worlds and make sense of their experiences.

'Big dreams' can initiate a change in some children's thinking and behaviour. It is natural for children to reflect upon their own behaviour, perhaps because they are being reprimanded by adults, are quietly concerned about their own jealousies or conflicts with siblings, and/ or as part of their moral development. Such thoughts can be revealed in dreams, as one boy experienced. John, aged 11, had been fighting with other children in school and was being regularly reprimanded by teachers. On one occasion John had hurt another boy – Josh – in a fight in the playground. Two days later, he dreamt that he was in the local scout hall where children were fighting. Josh appeared and hit John, knocking him to the ground. Josh placed one foot on John and stood on him with a clenched fist in the air 'like triumph... revenge' (Adams 2003, p.110).

John reflected upon his dream and found a meaning in it. In this case he believed the dream's message to be a warning that one day in a fight the opponent may be the victor. John explained that this (perceived) message led him to reconsider his aggressive behaviour in school and he subsequently approached Josh to apologise and asked him to become friends again. John was very honest about his behaviour since the dream and explained that 'I have tried hard not to get into fights. I can't say I haven't had any since the dream but I am trying harder.'

This example shows how it is important to listen to the child's response. It is tempting for adults to impose their own understanding of dreams on children, such as 'John was clearly worried about his own behaviour and this was evident in the dream.' Whilst this explanation may certainly largely account for the content of the dream, it does not acknowledge the pertinence of the dream to John. John could have reacted to the dream by simply seeing it as directly related to his behaviour in school. Instead he had found in it a deeper meaning – that he should apologise to Josh and change his own violent behaviour. John's reflections thus led to changes in his waking life and it is this response to the dream that has been crucial in giving the dream significance.

For some children the religious components of the dream are particularly meaningful. Maria, a 12-year-old girl, did not refer to an event occurring in her life at the time of her dream. However, the dream's content and her interpretations of it, indicate that she might have been concerned about issues of war and peace, although whether this had been a concern of psychological importance is difficult to determine from the data. Her dream was set in the midst of a war with the battleground being divided by a wall. She and other people were in the war zone and then jumped over the wall. This side of the wall was 'nice and peaceful' and they sat down with God in a circle and started praying whilst the battle raged on the other side. Maria described the dream as 'special', as one she 'had to remember'. Despite the potentially unsettling nature of the war scenes, this dream gave Maria a sense of reassurance. She was mature enough to know from news broadcasts that war is a feature of the waking world in which she lived and like many children her age, she worried that violent scenes observed in the media could potentially happen in her own city. However, Maria, like many children from religious and non-religious backgrounds alike, would at times turn to God for help. In this dream, she saw a man, whom she believed to be God, there to help resolve this particular battle. She felt that the dream could be a prediction of the future that 'God would be trying to make the world peaceful' (Adams 2003, p.111).

For Maria, her dream reflected her hope that the world would become less violent through God's intervention and to some extent confirmed it. The dream related closely to her Christian upbringing and whilst it expressed her fears over the violence seen in news coverage, it also gave her comfort that there could be a positive outcome for the world.

Dreaming of the deceased

Another common feature of children's dreams (as well as adults') is the appearance of people and pets known to them who have died. Psychologists including Barrett (1992) and Garfield (1996) have explored adults' dreams about deceased people who were close to the dreamer. Garfield (1996) studied these dreams over the course of the grieving period and identified a pattern that the dreams relating to the deceased followed. Towards the latter stages of the grieving period, a reassuring element is often apparent, for example with the deceased person appearing in the dream in realistic situations, bringing comfort to the dreamer. This comfort often takes the form of giving advice to the dreamer or reassuring the dreamer that they are still alive, albeit not in a physical form. Naturally, some of these dreams can be particularly pertinent and can occur in bereaved children as well as adults.

Claire is an 11-year-old girl whose friend Susie had died, three years prior to our meeting, when both of the girls had been eight years old. The dream came two-and-a-half years after the bereavement. In the dream Claire was walking through a large gold tunnel. At the end of the tunnel she saw Susie and they engaged in conversation about their lives. Susie explained that she was happy and had made new friends whilst Claire told her about events at school.

This dream made a positive impact upon Claire, in part shown by the fact that she had remembered this dream for half a year. She explained that the dream had made her feel happy because it had allowed her to see Susie again, and it had given her a sense of relief that Susie was 'alive and well' (Adams 2007). For children (as well as adults) such dreams can ease the grieving process, making them feel reconnected to the deceased person. In another case, seven-year-old Marshall described how he often dreamt of his deceased father talking to him, invariably giving advice about his school work. Marshall had been deeply distressed by his father's death from a sudden heart attack and as a result had become very unsettled at school, failing to concentrate on his work and disrupting others with poor behaviour. 'Daddy says [in my dreams] I need to, like, try hard at school, cos that would make him happy,' he explained. The offering of advice to the dreamer by the deceased is a typical feature of dreams during the grieving period.

Dreams and empathy

This chapter has highlighted the substantial amount of time which children spend in the dream state. Whilst no one remembers the majority of their dreams, some particularly significant ones are remembered and can be done so for a lifetime. Many children reflect upon their dreams, often of their own accord, and in some cases identify meanings in them. Yet many adults will be unaware of this, perhaps partly because they pay little attention to their own dreams which are so readily forgotten in the chaotic, busy lives that many lead. To adults such as these, who take little notice of their own dreams, the notion that many children do acknowledge their own may be a new idea. Children's lack of openness about their dreams is largely due to them being aware that some subjects are 'taboo'. A ten-year-old girl whom I interviewed said that she had not discussed her dreams with anyone before she spoke to me, in my capacity as a researcher. I asked her why not and she explained that she certainly hadn't mentioned them to her school friends because discussing dreams was 'uncool' (Adams *et al.* 2008).

Children have told researchers how they often do not talk about their dreams for fear of ridicule, disbelief or lack of interest. The common adult response of 'it's only a dream' can often be meant to be reassuring, but can be seen by children as not taking them seriously. The consequence of children's fears of such a reaction creates a cycle whereby children retreat into silence about their dreams and because adults do not hear about dreams, they do not ask the children about them, thus perpetrating a cycle of silence – a cycle which is also evident in children's unseen worlds as a whole.

Conversely, researchers who interview children about their dreams inevitably find many to be willing participants, eager to find an adult who is interested in their experiences. David Foulkes (1999) conducted the largest quantitative study of children's dreams which has occurred in a sleep laboratory and states that children make good subjects for dream research. One reason, he suggests, is that one of Freud and Jung's legacies is the suggestion that dreams are revealing of one's self which often leads adults to fear that if they disclose their dream, a researcher may identify hidden aspects of their personality. Conversely, children are not aware of this view and so tend to state their dreams in a matter-of-fact manner.

Whilst some children will choose not to disclose their dreams – which is to be respected – many will do so if only they are asked by an interested party. Yan, a Muslim boy whose family had fled a war in Eastern Europe to live in the UK, told me about a precognitive dream which had been significant for him. When I asked if he had told anyone about this dream he said, 'No,' and looked at me with a somewhat bemused expression as I asked him why not. He replied: 'No one asked me so I just didn't tell them. If somebody asked me I would tell them!'

This chapter has conveyed the common features of the dreamworlds into which children enter on a nightly basis: dreams of friends and family; of favourite characters from television; of glimpses into the future; dreams of the transcendent; and dreams of the deceased which are thought provoking. The children's responses to these dreams are varied, from mild interest to intrigue and fascination, from passing thoughts to deep reflections resulting in changes to thinking and behaviour. Dreams are worlds inhabited by children involuntarily, but are ones which can bring enjoyment, reassurance and curiosity.

Some recommendations

- Try to recall any dreams which have been particularly significant or memorable and consider the reasons for that impact. If you had them during childhood, try to recall how you understood the dream at the time and, if possible, whether or not that understanding has changed as you have entered adulthood.

- If you pay little attention to your dreams, or rarely remember them, try to focus on them for two or three weeks. There is a variety of methods for recording dreams and improving recall and you will need to find a method which best suits you. A common practice is to begin to keep a dream journal/diary which can be written or, if you prefer, an audio diary. If your recall is weak, mentally rehearse your intention to remember your dreams each night before you sleep and keep the pen and paper or recording device next to the bed in preparation to document anything you can remember. Upon awakening, *immediately* write down as much as you can remember, as this practice will stimulate your levels of recall. Pay particular attention to any emotions you experienced in the dream, give the dream a title and note any particular thoughts and reflections on what you have recalled. Bulkeley (2000) advises that it is important to focus on the quality of what you can remember and your reflections on it, rather than on the quantity of dreams. These activities will increase your awareness of your own dreams which in turn will generate greater empathy with children.

- If children begin to talk about their dreams, listen to them but do not judge them.

- Never attempt to interpret a child's dream, particularly in a professional setting, unless of course it is a clinical setting specifically using psychoanalytic methods and you are a qualified psychotherapist. Imposing your own meanings onto a child's (or an adult's) dream is to be firmly avoided at all costs; it is only the dreamer who can fully understand the meaning of their own dream because associations with symbols and imagery are intensely personal and will vary from one individual to another. Different cultural understandings will also bear upon any interpretation.

- If children begin to explain their understanding of the dream, which some will do independently, respect their attempts to make sense of their own experience.

- It is only by talking to children about their dream, and their understanding of it, that we can discover the insights which many children have. For example, whilst it would have been interesting to hear Ahmed's account of his dream of almost crashing into a tree whilst on his bike, there was much to be learnt about Ahmed and the way he makes sense of the world through discussion about the dream. It was only through that conversation that I learnt about his strong connection with Allah and his belief that Allah was not only protecting him, but also directly communicating through the dream. This discourse between adult and child strengthens the openness of the relationship and also builds trust, indicating to the child that the adult is genuinely interested in them and will listen without making judgements.

- Many children enjoy working with some of the dreams, for example drawing them or making a collage and this can be an enjoyable activity to share with them.

- Cultural factors can influence a child's willingness to talk about dreams and practitioners need to be mindful of each child's cultural heritage in this respect. For example, Fiske and Pillemer (2006) found that the Caucasian women they spoke to reported more frequent discussion about their dreams with their own parents than the Asian women in the same study (in an American context). In a religious context, Islam has tended to value dreams more highly than has Western Christianity, where dreams became demonised in the mediaeval period (see Bulkeley, Adams and Davis 2009). Hence, it is important to be mindful of the cultural norms which are influencing the conversation.

Children's dream-worlds can be fascinating, intriguing, comforting and sometimes significant. However, it would be wrong to imply that children's dream-worlds all fall into positive categories. On the contrary, key characteristics of children's dream lives are the 'dark' components. They can bring the undesirable elements of the television programmes, the anxieties of waking life and the feared characters of children's fairy stories into their nightly worlds in the form of nightmares. The following chapter enters this 'dark' aspect of the night alongside the other more frightening facets of children's worlds.

CHAPTER 5

The darker worlds

There is a risk that children's unseen worlds can be seen through rose-tinted glasses: that adults may think of them in romanticised terms, envisioning blissful worlds untouched by the harsh realities of 'real' life. To some extent, at least for those who are fortunate enough to enjoy a high quality of life in all that may entail, childhood can be seen as a protected, relatively carefree period of life in which the young participate in creative, playful worlds with seemingly limitless boundaries. The children's experiences charted in the preceding chapters may, if read in isolation, support that notion and convey a one-sided portrayal of children's worlds as places of harmony and creativity. Certainly, most appear to embody those qualities, but not all do so. On the contrary, some worlds can be unsettling or even frightening places and these demand attention because, although fewer in number than the enchanting worlds, they exist and children need more support from adults in understanding and managing them. This chapter explores the darker worlds which many children inhabit at times. Continuing the theme of night, it begins with the enemy of dreams – the terrifying world of nightmares – before moving into the darker side of some of the worlds already visited and considering the impact of the fears they can instil in children.

Nightmares
Nightmares could be described as the most visible world of those which children enter at night; 'visible' in the sense that observers are more aware of their nightmares than they are of their dreams. Children's reactions to them – of awaking screaming in terror – gives them an immediate presence and urgency for both children and those

around them. In attempts to console, parents/carers naturally ask what has happened and children usually retell their stories. There is no doubt that they had entered a frightening world and need a little time to become calm and recognise that they are at home in their bed and not in the midst of the danger-scene depicted in the nightmare.

Research into the dream lives of children consistently shows that nightmares are a regular and normal feature of childhood dreaming, and usually decrease in frequency in adolescence (Woolley and Wellman 1992). Mallon cites reports of nightmares from children, many of whom encounter them at some stages of their life between the ages of three and 16 (Mallon 1989, 2002), with the highest concentration occurring between the ages of four and six (Hartmann 1996, Siegel and Bulkeley 1998). Siegel and Bulkeley (1998) emphasise the 'normality' of nightmares, stating that they play a role in coping with changes in life, such as beginning school, moving house or parents' divorce.

Similar themes in nightmares recur across different studies and typically include being chased, attacked or being in another type of threatening situation. In Mallon's (2002) study, children reported the following general themes:

- fear of separation;
- fear of being abandoned;
- being injured and attacked;
- 'shapeshifting' dreams in which a non-threatening character changed form into a frightening one.

One of the key differences between adults and children's dreams is that the latter include a much higher number of animals. However, these animals are often wild and adopt an aggressive role, usually attacking the child. Siegel and Bulkeley (1998, p. 39) cite the dream of Amy, an eight-year-old American girl who said 'in my dream it really sounded like a wolf and a pig were snorting down either side of my head; it sounded like they were going to eat me up'.

Given that dreams reflect our thoughts, emotions and experiences of the present and the past, it is unsurprising that negative images from the waking world emerge in nightmares, transporting them into terrifying worlds. Children who live in war zones understandably report nightmares related to the context in which they live, as Punamäki (1999) exemplifies in a study of 125 Palestinian children (80 living in conditions of political violence in the Gaza Strip and 45 in the peaceful town of Galilee in Israel) and 80 Finnish children living in Helsinki. The children, aged 7–12, completed dream and sleep diaries for one week. The findings unsurprisingly showed that the Palestinian children living in the violent area reported more persecution and aggression dreams than the children living in the two peaceful areas. Negative imagery included scenes of injury, hostility, aggression and emotions such as sadness and fear.

Similarly, children living in Northern Ireland in times of terrorist attacks reported nightmares which reflected the conflict. Orla, an 11-year-old girl, told Mallon (2002, p.146):

> I dreamt that I woke up to go to the toilet and I heard a ticking noise downstairs. I went down and realised it was a bomb. I started screaming and woke everybody up. They all came downstairs and got out of the house before it blew up.

However it is not only children who live in war-torn countries who inhabit nightmare worlds. With access to the media, internet and computer games, children are regularly exposed to graphic images of wars around the globe as well as other forms of violence, both fictional and non-fictional, which re-emerge in their nightmares. I spoke to Rachel, a Scottish ten-year-old girl from a Christian background, who explained that she had a recurring nightmare in which God kept changing into the devil and then back into His own form. When He appeared as the devil, destruction ensued, but when He appeared as God, He ushered people onto a bus for protection. She was clear about the source of her nightmare, saying 'I'd watched a film like that. I think it was a film where the devil was giving these cards out to people after they'd died'. In addition, other fears which children have, which are not necessarily connected directly to the media, such as being separated from their family, can also emerge in their nightmares. In Mallon's (2002) study, children often reported nightmares which contained images directly from videos and television programmes they had seen at home. Kane, a six-year-old boy, had a recurring nightmare about a monster's head being sawn off with an electric saw which stemmed from a video he had watched with his parents. Kane became afraid of going to sleep because of its recurring nature.

How 'real' are nightmares to children? The answer is, in short, very real, just as they are to adults who experience them. For anyone, irrespective of their age, this is a distressing experience. For children it can be even more so, especially for the very young who find it difficult to understand the explanations offered to them. When nightmares are regular, sometimes with the same one recurring, children can become increasingly anxious during waking hours and worry about going to sleep for fear that the nightmare will return. Parents/carers can misinterpret a child's protests about going to bed as them being awkward and whilst that is certainly the case some of the time, there will be other instances when the child is genuinely reluctant to go to sleep for fear of entering nightmare worlds. Practical advice on supporting children through their nightmares will be given in chapter 8.

Other fears of the night

Darkness naturally enhances a person's fear because it immediately limits the ability to see clearly, creating anxieties about what may or may not be lurking in the shadows. Consequently children's fears of the dark are not merely limited to the nightmare episodes of sleep, but can also be present whilst they are awake. Morris and Kratochwill (1983) suggest that fear of the dark often manifests itself around the age of three and can last until the age of eight. At the age of four this fear of the dark can be accompanied by a fear of noises at night, and from the ages of six to eight, a fear of supernatural beings is also common.

For many children the house or bedroom can be completely transformed by the darkness into worlds inhabited by monsters and other threatening creatures or beings which hover in hidden corners. The gentle tapping of a branch against the window becomes an entity which is hammering through the glass to break into the room whilst a shadow of a toy bear cast onto the wall becomes a gigantic monster seeking out his prey. These dark worlds are different from the scary scenarios which children like to create in their fantasy play. In these play settings, many children enjoy battling terrorising monsters, witches or ghosts as they run and scream. Sandra, mother of four-year-old Ben, often watches her son and his friends playing such games. She explained,

> It's quite amazing really, how the children seem to create this entire land of dinosaurs who have come back from the past. Mostly the dinosaurs seem to be aggressive and carnivorous and determined to eat the children for dinner. The noise from the children shouting and squealing can be deafening, you would certainly believe they are really terrified yet they seem to enjoy it all at the same time. Sometimes I watch them finding solutions such as sending the dinosaurs back in time, killing them with special dinosaur lasers or feeding them pieces of meat to satisfy their appetites. Then, in a flash, the screaming stops and the children's fear is suddenly gone and they move on to another activity.

At other times however, Ben is fearful of the dark, believing that 'something' is in his bedroom. How is it, then, that a child like Ben can simultaneously fear a monster which they believe is in the room whilst also fearing one which they have willingly created for the purposes of play?

Harris (2000), writing on the imagination, considers possible reasons for children's reactions of fear to imaginary entities and reflects on two alternative explanations. First, he draws the analogy between adults' responses to watching a film which initiates a quickening of the heart rate at a dramatic point such as the heroine entering alien territory. The observer of the film knows that the dangers ahead of her are entirely fictitious but the imaginary premises drive the emotional system nonetheless. It may be that children respond in a similar way, knowing the difference between what he terms fantasy and reality, but because emotion can be activated by material in either domain, they nevertheless experience fear.

In a second explanation, Harris (2000) considers that children can create an imaginary entity such as a monster, and then elaborate on their invention, beginning to react as if the fictitious premises were literally true. The created scenario thus begins to be treated as an emotionally charged actuality. According to this theory, children may be aware that the monster lurking in the shadows is purely imaginary even though they are reacting with fear, just as adults do when they

have watched a horror film and decide to sleep with the light on…
just in case. Implicit in these theories are the concepts of 'reality and
fantasy' and, as they are highly applicable to all of the children's
worlds described in this book, a more detailed discussion of them will
be offered in chapters 7 and 9.

The threat of the unseen

Not all threatening encounters occur during the darkness. Indeed,
some take place in broad daylight but can remain unseen to the adult
eye. Chapter 3 described some of the amiable invisible companions
who accompany children in their daily lives, often giving friendly
advice or being reliable playmates. However, whilst the vast majority
of companions are a pleasure to have around, not all are so benign.
At best, these less pleasant companions are a source of annoyance
(Hallowell 2007). Taylor (1999, p.19) cites children who complained,
'she puts yoghurt in my hair', 'he hits me on the head,' and 'she won't
share'. Others constantly make negative comments and criticisms,
some bite children, others have temper tantrums and some are simply
frustrating because they will not go away. It could, of course, be argued
that these behaviours are typical features of any childhood friendship.

Hallowell (2007) uncovered a more unusual account when he
talked to Sharon, mother of an eight-year-old boy called Lewis who
had a companion named Douglas, all of whom lived in a farmhouse.
At the age of three Lewis could often be heard talking even when
there was no one else there but Sharon thought little of it. However,
she began to notice unusual occurrences in the house such as items
going missing and reappearing several days later, hearing tapping
noises at the back door and pennies appearing from nowhere. One
day, when Lewis was five years old, Sharon was talking to her mother
in their living room, when they heard a terrifying scream from Lewis.
The women raced upstairs to find Lewis lying on the floor covered by
a huge pile of clothes with Lewis insisting that he had been attacked
by Douglas. Lewis was able to describe Douglas as a seven-year-old
boy who wore 'grey shorts, a white shirt and a funny flat cap', who
had died in an accident on the farm when he had fallen asleep in a
hay mound and, hidden from view, his father had unwittingly thrust
a pitchfork into the mound. Overall, Sharon described Douglas as

harmless but he would often open drawers and cupboards and pull the family's hair (Hallowell 2007, p. 46).

The account of Douglas seems to overlap with the popular conception of a ghost, in the sense that the spirit of the person who has died remains in the same place and conveys their presence in various ways. Whilst Lewis' mother did not appear to be too distressed by the occurrences, some seemingly inexplicable events can be frightening for all concerned as Hart (2003) illustrates with a mother's narration of a troubling event with her toddler son. She used to pull him on a sledge as they did not have a car. The boy thoroughly enjoyed riding on it but one day they went down a small road that they had not travelled down before. Part way down the road her son started to scream, rolled off the sledge and refused to get back on. His anxiety was intense and his behaviour most unusual and his mother could not console him. Eventually she decided to turn around and go back, at which point he got back on the sledge and continued the journey quite happily. The following day his mother described the incident to his babysitter who explained that 30 or 40 years earlier a child had been killed on that road whilst sledging. The explanation for the young boy's tantrum at this point on the road is, of course, open to speculation but the incident was clearly distressing for both him and his mother.

Other dark encounters may be more unusual. Dash (1997) compiled accounts of strange phenomena, mostly from adults, but with some interesting cases from children and teenagers. He details that of Randy, a Californian teenager, who returned to his home one day at the age of 13 to see a small, pot-bellied creature sitting in an armchair. It was roughly two feet tall, jet black, had red circles for eyes, pointed ears and two small white fangs. Randy walked towards it as the creature looked at him but when Randy blinked, it vanished. A few months later Randy saw it again sitting cross-legged on a shelf in his bedroom grinning at him before disappearing again. Some years later, when Randy was at college reading in bed with the lights on, he sensed something entering the room by coming through the wall above his head. This time it was invisible but Randy heard the sound of leathery, bat-like wings and sensed it flying across the room and out through the opposite wall.

Empathising with children's fears

Recalling our own childhood fears can go some way to seeing the children's darker worlds through their eyes, although the adult lenses through which we see them can make it difficult to fully comprehend. Jersild and Holmes (2007) asked 303 adults to describe their earliest fears recollected from their own childhood. The largest category, cited by 23.5 per cent of the sample, was a fear of the darkness, being alone in the dark or imaginary events occurring in the dark. A further 4.7 per cent remembered fear of the supernatural and imaginary creatures other than those specifically mentioned in the first category.

Hermann, now in his 30s, laughed as he described how he used to be terrified of an area in a public playground near his home.

> The playground was a wide open space with swings, a slide and a couple of climbing frames. There were no hidden parts where anyone could hide, but there was just one corner of it which was covered in grass where all my friends used to play football but I just wouldn't go near. When I was about four, I remember screaming as my dad told me to stop being silly and just join in with my friends' game, but there was something about that area that just freaked me out to the point where I wouldn't go to it. I don't remember why, all I remember is this intense fear, and I always managed to avoid playing in that part, not that anything bad ever happened to my friends who played there. It was all very strange.

That corner of the playground seemed different somehow. Hermann cannot remember *why* he felt it was so prohibitive, just the feelings he had and his physical reaction to them of refusing to enter that part of the playground. He asked his father about his recollections of it but his father said that Hermann had never explained why, and that his response had almost seemed instinctive. It is impossible to fully recollect our own fears of childhood, particularly as they are now subject to adult filters which can diminish their intensity and seek logical explanations, but it is important to at least attempt to understand children's fears through their eyes.

Acknowledging children's darker worlds

Morris and Kratochwill (1983) point out that every human being experiences fear and in children it is part of their normal development. Many fears are transitory and do not significantly interfere with their daily lives. Children's fears are wide-ranging and include fears of injury/harm, separation from the primary caregiver, animals (Morris and Kratochwill 1983, Sorin 2003) and loud noises, strangers and changes in their environment (Morris and Kratochwill 1983). Naturally, children living in war zones or other traumatic situations will also experience particular fears pertinent to their context.

For many adults, it is common to avoid talking about potentially distressing experiences, whether it is death, serious illness, divorce, accidents, paedophilia or other criminal acts. Avoidance of such topics can be seen as a natural human reaction, sometimes an aspect of denial that they even exist, serving as a form of coping mechanism. When children are experiencing fears such as those described in this chapter, adults need to offer support to them and acknowledge the intensity of their feelings. Naturally, a child's anguish unsettles adults who care for them. Adults can become frustrated if the child does not accept their reassurances that there is no monster in the bedroom, or that 'there is no such things as ghosts'. What the adult perceives to be a rational explanation is not always understood in the same way by the frightened child. The situation can be further complicated where there is uncertainty on behalf of the adult, for example if a bizarre event occurs which might lend itself to a supernatural explanation and the adult finds it difficult to provide an alternative reason. Chapter 8 offers practical advice for helping children to cope with the frightening aspects of unseen worlds.

Some recommendations

- Encounters with darker worlds are inevitable and children need a voice to express them just as much as they need a voice to express their more magical, enjoyable worlds.

- It is natural for children to experience fear and it is important that adults help children to manage and understand their fears even though it may be tempting to ignore them because it is easier to do so. The role of the practitioner in giving support will vary according to that role. For example, it may be within the remit and training of some counsellors or those working with traumatised children in other care settings. Nursery and teaching staff are often required to undertake tasks relating to exploring children's feelings as part of programmes of personal and social development and well-being. However, practitioners who are not qualified counsellors should avoid attempting to take on a therapeutic role. Should they be worried by children's accounts, they should inform the parents/carers.

- Whilst children's fears are a normal part of being human, those relating to the darker elements of their worlds need to be acknowledged if the child raises them. Rationalising the scenarios is a natural response but simple explanations such as 'monsters do not exist' can be ineffective as they do not acknowledge the fear that the child is experiencing. Instead, consider alternative strategies which support the child in taking responsibility for finding a solution (see suggestions in chapter 8).

- Whilst nightmares are a normal part of childhood, some children may be suffering from post-traumatic nightmares and these need to be referred to a specialist counsellor.

- Children need to express their fears, either through discussion or other means such as drawing or writing as they can find it difficult to make sense of them independently. Be alert to children who need to express them and, if appropriate, inform their parents/carers.

- Do not dismiss or trivialise a child's fears. Be aware that your adult lenses may tell you that is simply imagination, but to a child it is very real.

As the preceding chapters have shown, children inhabit a range of worlds, playful, creative, mysterious and sometimes frightening. The ways in which adults react to children's encounters can have significant effects upon them, and attention now turns to the range of ways in which adults respond and the effects that those reactions can have upon children.

CHAPTER 6

It's just your imagination

Jennifer described how her parents had raised her in the 1960s. They had set strict boundaries but also spent much time playing with her and teaching her how to read and write before she began school. She had nice toys but wasn't spoilt, and was encouraged to make friends with other children. Like all children with younger siblings she occasionally fought and argued with them but overall they enjoyed amicable relations. To the observer, Jennifer had a happy childhood in the midst of a loving and caring family, but she spent much of it feeling sad, something which went unnoticed by her parents. A major factor in contributing to these negative feelings was a sense that her parents never particularly took her seriously especially when she talked about the nightmares which frightened her and the mysterious figures she saw around her bed which comforted her. Jennifer explained:

> I used to get upset because my mum and dad just seemed to dismiss anything I said, although as an adult now I can understand why. As a kid, I always had my head in books about ghosts and the supernatural in a bid to explain my own experiences, but my parents just said that I read too much and I had an overactive imagination. They didn't realise that actually, when I read these books, I didn't feel alone because I knew that the authors and the people they described in them had similar experiences to me. The truth is, I could turn to these books but I couldn't turn to my parents. To this day I honestly don't think they realise I felt that they didn't take me seriously.

This chapter begins to explore the wide range of adults' responses to children's involvement in the unseen worlds – both positive and negative – and how their reactions affect children. Thus far, some of the accounts included have been offered by adults who have been referring to childhoods from earlier decades, which may have had different social constructions surrounding them. This chapter begins with an exploration of the wider context of childhood before focusing on how contemporary notions of childhood affect adults' responses to children's worlds.

Contemporary childhood and children's rights

As noted in chapter 1, given that the concept of childhood is not purely a matter of biology and physiology alone, but is also in part a social construction, our concept of what constitutes childhood is a fluid one which changes over time and across cultures (Stainton Rogers 2003, James *et al.* 2006). In many of today's industrialised societies such as the UK children have a strong presence, becoming increasingly visible in a variety of ways, both positive and negative, and have entire industries being created around them. Manufacturers, sellers, advertisers and the media have combined to systematically target children as consumers in their own right, no longer just providing simple toys and comics for them, but an almost infinite array of products including sophisticated electronic toys, laptop computers, mobile phones, clothes, music CDs as well as junk food. The newly created 'tweenies/tweens', aged 7 to 12, increasingly show teenage tendencies, largely through such consumerist choices (Waller 2005).

Children's visibility in Western societies has not increased simply through a high media and consumerist profile, but also through a series of cultural changes which include a growing range of legal rights for young people. The children's rights movement has a long history, with the first formal Declaration of the Rights of the Child being made in 1924 in order to support children who had lost homes and families during the First World War (Rudduck and Flutter 2000). Other advances were made in the following decades but the most notable, contemporary influence came from the United Nations Convention on the Rights of the Child in 1989 (UNCRC). This gave children the same rights as adults in addition to specific rights that acknowledge their vulnerability. In so doing, the UNCRC viewed children's rights in terms of four 'Ps':

- Provision rights which enable children's growth and development, including rights to food, housing and education;

- Prevention rights – systems which can prevent the abuse of children or infringement of their rights including providing legal representation for them;

- Protection rights which protect them against exploitation and abuse and intervention if their rights have been infringed;

- Participation rights which allow children a voice in decisions made on their behalf.

(Burr and Montgomery 2003, p. 144)

The UNCRC was ratified by the majority of countries in the world (although it was not without its critics) and has subsequently given children rights which have never previously been seen. These include the right to freedom of expression (Article 13) and the right to thought, conscience and religion (Article 14) (Handley 2005). Many countries then legislated for these rights, for example, in England and Wales this was achieved largely through the Children Act 1989 and the Children Act 2004. The child's voice now has a high profile in many public arenas in the UK including social policy, child protection and education. The Education system has witnessed an increasing emphasis on the child's voice with the (then) Department for Education and Skills (DfES) incorporating it into the curriculum (see DfES 2004). A rise was seen in the number of formal forums in schools, such as pupil councils, which has given them an opportunity to express their views on how their school should be run. This increase in participation gained further momentum when Parliament passed a law in November 2008 which will require all schools to consult pupils on a vast range of issues including teaching, learning and behaviour (Stewart 2009). This recent move has met with both approval and concern from various teachers and trade unions but demonstrates what can be seen as a significant cultural and political shift in attitudes towards childhood and children. Yet in other countries such as Denmark, the child's voice has been given a much more prominent position for many years. Klein (2003) argues that Denmark has the most radical democratic structure in its schools compared to other European countries. There, teaching and learning take place in a dialogic culture and two student representatives are elected to sit on a board of governors. Thus the status of the child's voice will vary across cultures as well as across different historical periods and it is important to be conscious of this contextual information when reflecting on how we respond to children.

As children are being given a more prominent place in many Western cultures, they are simultaneously more able to negotiate and construct their own place in society. Children's attitudes and views are not only heard in formal contexts such as school councils or child protection panels, but also on a daily basis in informal contexts such as shops ('I want that toy') and the home ('why do I have to eat my dinner? I want my ice cream'). In many cases, the child's requests or demands are unsolicited whilst in others, adults actively seek their preferences and views. However, irrespective of the context, many children are increasingly able to express, question and challenge what adults say whether it be done respectfully or disrespectfully. In fact, the National Curriculum in schools in England and Wales actively invites children to reflect, question and debate and teachers are expected to encourage children to express and share their views on a wide range of issues including those of a personal, social and emotional nature.

Given this rise in prominence of the child's voice, it is easy for adults to assume that children will naturally express their thoughts and feelings, even without being invited to at times. However, this is a dangerous assumption to make when considering the types of experiences detailed in this book, because there are various factors at work which can lead children to retreat into silence about unseen worlds, particularly as they grow older.

Growing up too soon?

There is a strong concern in some industrialised nations that children are growing up too quickly. Such fears from different sectors of society, including parents/carers and practitioners working with children in various fields, are entirely understandable in the context of the increasing sexualisation of children, especially of young girls. The 'tween' market arouses particular concern when girls are targeted with cosmetics, skimpy clothes and magazines that talk explicitly of sexual relationships. The media's emphasis on celebrity culture which appears to value stick-thin physiques has raised fears that it is contributing to the rise in numbers of children developing eating disorders in desperate bids to remain under their natural body weight. Adults in the West are naturally worried about the pressure from society and peers on young children to grow up too quickly. Practitioners and parents/carers in particular have a vested interest in ensuring that children do not suffer from the dangerous consequences of society's pressure on them to 'grow up' too soon (these potentially include early sexual relations, sexually transmitted diseases, teenage pregnancy, eating disorders, drinking alcohol or drug taking, making uninformed choices about consumer purchases, etc.). At the same time children need to be accepted by their peers and need to conform to their peer group, which may be at odds with their parents' expectations. Parents/carers also want to see their children mature, and take pleasure in doing so, and will encourage them to develop their decision-making skills.

These tensions also affect children's participation in their multiple worlds. Being conscious of wanting to grow up and being under the influence of the media and peer pressure to do so, children in the tween stage of life begin to increasingly identify themselves with the teenage world. In particular, this process involves actively disassociating themselves with what they perceive to be childish behaviour and ideas, which can include many aspects of the unseen worlds.

These are the worlds of *young* children…

Most adults associate worlds of fantasy play, fairies, Santa Claus, monsters and ghosts with small children – a notion which filters down to the children themselves. Consequently, children also come to equate these concepts with younger children, particularly evidenced in their attempts (or otherwise!) to conceal from their younger siblings that Santa Claus doesn't really exist and that their parents are in fact the bearers of gifts each year. No longer believing in Santa Claus is possibly one of the many contributing factors which enable children to feel that they are no longer 'little' and are nearing the world of teenagers and adulthood. They quickly realise that Western society deems fairy tales, magic spells and make-believe as the fanciful realm of young children, namely the period of life through which they have progressed.

Children will naturally question their beliefs in the light of new experiences and new information as they grow. For example, when children hear claims that Santa Claus does not exist, or that the ghost they saw was just a trick of the light they will automatically consider these statements in the light of their own experience and other knowledge. With regards to Santa Claus, they may begin to wonder how it can be physically possible to travel around the world in one night when they have learnt that it will take 24 hours on an aeroplane to fly from London to Sydney, on the opposite side of the world with only one stop being made to refuel. They might also have realised that some people dress up as Santa Claus which can make the problem of determining which is the 'real' Santa Claus somewhat more complex – if indeed possible at all. Adults' association of unseen worlds with younger children creates particular difficulties for older children who learn to make this connection. In turn, the association also naturally shapes adults' responses, which will be considered shortly.

These are also the worlds of older children…

However, research in a variety of disciplines suggests that it is not just very young children who believe in the worlds covered in this book. Unfortunately, many older children have chosen to remain silent about their beliefs and experiences, in part because of their widespread association with younger children.

Chapter 3 explored the intriguing world of imaginary companions. Historically these were considered to be the domain of pre-school children but various studies have demonstrated that some older children, adolescents and even adults also have them. Taylor (1999, p.135) cites the work of Seiffge-Krenke, a developmental psychologist, who analysed diary entries of 241 children and adolescents for references to imaginary companions. These were mentioned in 35 per cent of the diaries of 11 to 13-year-olds, 55 per cent of those of 14- and 15-year-olds, and 28 per cent of those written by 16- and 17-year-olds. Similarly, when Hoff (2004) interviewed ten-year-olds about their imaginary companions, she noted how many felt awkward and giggled, implying that it was embarrassing to believe in them. She cited Harald, a Swedish boy, who explained during the taped interview that he had stopped having make-believe friends when he was seven but once the tape was turned off, he revealed that he had in fact played with his friend during the summer holiday. Harald was clearly apprehensive about what his classmates might say if they knew that he still retained his imaginary companion when they claimed they no longer had theirs.

Amongst the group of children I spoke to, belief in both ghosts and invisible friends was actually higher in the older age group (aged 8–11) than it was in the younger age group (aged 4–7). Whilst the figures for belief in fairies was higher amongst the younger children (60%, n=12), it was not as low as one might have anticipated in the older group, with 45 per cent (n=9) still believing in some form of fairy (the tooth fairy being a prominent figure about whom the children initiated discussion). Like Harald, in the Swedish study, some of the older children in my group were acutely aware of age-related expectations of others. Henry, aged eight, said 'as you get older they say you don't believe as much, but I still believe.' Kascey, aged nine, explained that 'usually when you're young you have an imaginary friend'. Leah echoed her thoughts, saying 'I used to have an imaginary friend, but I've just kind of grown out of it.' Later in the conversation I detected some reluctance to accept this expectation of letting go, when Leah mentioned 'Now my dad has given me a teddy so I do things with him now, like talk to him and play with him' instead of with her imaginary friend.

Adults' responses to children's worlds

Whilst responses to children vary according to the context and to each individual adult's outlook, children report similarities in the reactions they receive. Children who hear largely affirmative responses from certain people will inevitably continue such conversations with those same people, but they will be aware that the same positivity will not be found with all audiences. The consequence is that they, like most adults, will simply be selective about whom they tell, which is a good life skill to possess. The disheartening news is that many children (and indeed some adults) do not feel that they can tell anyone, with the exception of the researchers to whom they are making their first declaration – on the understanding that their identity will be concealed in any dissemination of the findings. What types of responses do children typically receive?

POSITIVE RESPONSES
When children are young others around them, both children and adults, naturally engage with their play and imagination and often actively participate with them. This participation can take different forms according to the context. When children's fantasy play is the activity concerned, others become involved by either providing props or direction to support it. In a formal setting such as a nursery or a school adults may construct a corner of the room to facilitate this type of play. One week the corner may be a doctor's surgery, the next it becomes a travel agent's and the week after that it may be a kitchen. These changes become equipped with the appropriate furniture, clothes, toys or props to facilitate the transformations which help children to become immersed in these different roles.

On other occasions, young children may spontaneously offer insights into their activities. If a five-year-old enters the room and declares that she has been at a fairies' tea party in the corner of the garden, a typical response would be to smile and comment, 'That sounds lovely. What did you eat?' These affirmations of young children's worlds are made instinctively as adults are naturally interested and engage with the children to share in their excitement and encourage learning/vocabulary etc. Such involvement is clearly highly supportive for children, but tends to be restricted to younger children with whom play and imagination are more widely associated. More detail, together with advice on holding such conversations with children, follows in chapter 8.

LESS HELPFUL RESPONSES
From children's perspectives, it does not necessarily take an outright dismissal such as 'stop being silly' to silence their sharing of the unseen. Other responses, particularly fleeting ones, are equally potentially detrimental. Anwar, a nine-year-old boy, suggested that his mother was a very polite woman with a habit of smiling.

I used to tell her that I could see these tiny little lights hovering in the corner of my room, sort of jumping up and down, like they wanted to play with me. I didn't know what they were, you know, but when I say about them my mum just says 'oh that's nice' and smiles at me. She keeps doing her jobs when I tell her. I think she is always busy.

Anwar's frustration lay in the fact that his mother did not engage in conversation with him. Although her reply was not explicitly dismissive, it expressed a lack of interest; a lack of desire to know more.

Naturally, some adults have little interest in exploring children's worlds, particularly as the children grow older, but even those who do can face the problem of scarcity of time. The early morning scenario in family households is easily recognisable. Parents/carers frantically try to organise reluctant children to get dressed and eat their breakfast, settle squabbles between siblings, whilst simultaneously planning their own duties for the day – all to very tight time schedules. The notion of sitting eating a leisurely family breakfast around the kitchen table can feel like an unobtainable fantasy drawn from a 1950s' film set. If a child were to start describing a dream or nightmare which was still vivid in their mind, there may be a strong possibility that the adults will not be able to give it due care and attention in the midst of the hectic environment. For the child, this can feel as if the adults are not interested.

In a professional setting similar scenarios can arise. In a classroom with 29 other children and numerous learning objectives to be fulfilled in each lesson, teachers and teaching assistants can also struggle to find the time to devote to conversations with individual children. When adults are unable to respond affirmatively, children may not appreciate that this is due to other pressures and can interpret the lack of response as an indication of a lack of interest. Of course in some cases they are right!

RESPONSES TO DARKER WORLDS
Adults' responses to a child's descriptions of their darker worlds can be particularly problematic because the child may be in distress. An adult can be anxious when they encounter a child who is suffering

from fears of a monster hiding in the cupboard, or is too afraid to sleep because of the mad axe-man who will chase them around the house in their nightmares. One of the most natural and spontaneous responses is, 'don't worry, the monster doesn't really exist, it's just your imagination' or 'don't worry, there is no axe-man, it's only a dream'. These statements are delivered with complete sincerity and are underlined by a desire to reassure and comfort the child. After all, the adult knows that the cupboard is filled with clothes and toys and is certainly not inhabited by a monster. Similarly, there is no axe-man chasing the child around the house because he is simply a product of the random neurons in the child's brain which are firing during the sleep state. It is thus natural to offer children these scientific/rational perspectives in order to teach them about the workings of the mind and hopefully ease their fears so that they may once again open their cupboard door without thinking and look forward to a good night's sleep, thereby transforming their places of fear into safe spaces.

However, for many children these responses do not chase away the entities. From their worldview the monster is very present; it lives and breathes in the cupboard; the child can hear it moving in the quiet hours of the night; the child can see the traces of where it has walked, as its tail has knocked over their plastic tower blocks which had been stacked in the far corner of the cupboard. From their perspective the axe-man is completely authentic; he comes to terrify them as they sleep in their bed, causing them to awake in utter terror screaming for their parents to rescue them. The axe-man is determined to return several nights a week to persistently and systematically subject them to a terrifying chase. These children *know* that these creatures are real and little their parents can say can console them. Stating that 'it's just your imagination' may serve to inadvertently belittle the child's experience, almost brushing it aside as if it were meaningless and unworthy of attention. A child may become increasingly worried if they feel that their parents/carers are not taking them sufficiently seriously and may retreat into themselves, becoming even more fearful of the terror inherent in shadowy spaces. This scenario is exemplified by Kara, an eight-year-old girl who described her situation to me.

> I don't like going to bed cos I keep hearing something underneath my bed, like a big creature or something like that.

When it's late and I've heard Mum and Dad go to their bedroom and the television is off so there is no noise in the house, then I hear the deep breaths of this animal that is under my bed. I haven't seen it but he must be big because he breathes so loud and I can sometimes hear him move and bump into my toys I keep there. I'm so scared he will come out one day and bite me so I don't like to sleep a lot in case he comes when I am asleep.

I asked what happens when the animal comes and she told me that she would scream for her father to come and get rid of it, but he thought that she was just 'trying to stay up later' and didn't believe her when she told him that the animal was there.

Kara's parents had tried to support her by looking under the bed to make certain that there were no animals there and also by offering other explanations for the noises, such as the pipes settling down when the central heating was turned off. But no alternative reasons could satisfy Kara's quest for answers and her parents felt helpless, hoping that she would 'grow out of' the notion that there was something living under her bed. The anxieties of both adults and children which are involved in matters of children's darker worlds demand more detailed attention and practical strategies which will be given in chapter 8 when exploring how adults can affirm children's worlds.

The hidden nature of children's unseen worlds

This chapter has considered how adults respond to children's accounts of unseen worlds and has viewed some of these responses in the light of cultural conceptions of childhood. It has become evident that many well-intentioned responses such as 'it's just your imagination' can lead to children feeling that they are not being taken seriously. This is an important issue because it can not only damage children's self-esteem, but it can also have a prolonged effect on them, lasting into adulthood, making them feel that others do not always value what they say. Such feelings, when related to the matter of unseen worlds, can be exacerbated in societies which do not inherently value these types of beliefs and experiences.

In order to develop empathy with children when considering how responses affect them, consider similar scenarios from an adult's perspective. Bill, an engineer, exemplifies how few people will initiate topics of conversation in which their audience has no interest, or are likely to ridicule.

> I've ploughed through the vast literature on alien abductions and there certainly is a lot of deluded rubbish out there, but if you are critical and weed that out, you find some seriously thought-provoking stuff. Some of the testimonies have come from high ranking ex-government officials who have tired of keeping this controversial phenomenon secret. But when I bring the subject up, it generally just meets with laughter. My mates just took the mickey, saying I needed to see a psychiatrist and accusing me of watching too much science fiction, so I no longer raise it, except with my cousin who takes it pretty seriously.

Bill's search for a sympathetic audience is a natural human reaction. He is actively avoiding ridicule and seeking dialogue with people who share his passion for the subject and who will be non-judgemental even if they disagree with his ideas. Children are no different. In my earlier research on significant dreams, many children said that they had initially told their parents, but as they had not believed them, they had not tried to talk about dreams again. In those households, dreams moved out of view as the children no longer mentioned them and their parents never enquired further.

The chances of children feeling misunderstood in relation to the unseen worlds can increase as they become older. The tween stage causes confusion for young people as to what they should or should not believe now that they are growing older, and also causes confusion for adults who can become uncertain about how to react to children who appear to grasp on to their beliefs which are increasingly classified as childish.

'I didn't tell anyone because…'

When children perceive adults' responses to be dismissive or uninterested, irrespective of whether or not that perception is accurate, older children are particularly prone to repressing their experiences, and understandably so. Adults' responses to children's worlds are linked into wider cultural attitudes which can also make a considerable impact on children's willingness to share them. Writing on religion and spirituality in the West, Hay (1985, p.140) interviewed adults and found that many people, especially males, are reluctant to share their spiritual experiences because the West has a 'suspicion of the spiritual'. One of the consequences is that these types of experiences which are disclosed to researchers are often kept hidden from those with whom they interact on a daily basis. Similarly in Canada, Scott (2004, p. 68) gathered 22 adults' recollections of spiritual experiences encountered in childhood and adolescence. He observed that most of his participants had never shared their experience before. He writes, 'Even though the experience was significant and influential in a person's life, the story has remained private.'

Hay (1985) and Scott's (2004) findings from adult surveys bear similarities to those undertaken with children which suggest that young people are very much aware of societal taboos, quickly realising what is acceptable to talk about and what is not, in the context of their age and social groups. In my conversations with children about unseen worlds, several were quick to explain why they had been careful about whom they told. In chapter 3 Caitlin described her invisible friend Poppy who played, chatted and ate with her. Given that Caitlin's parents provided a plastic plate for Poppy when they ate outside in the garden, Caitlin was clearly comfortable talking about this aspect of her life with them. However, further conversation revealed that Caitlin, like most children, was selective about whom she told. Her parents were clearly understanding of Caitlin's experience, but she was highly aware that others would not be. She had told two friends but not the rest of her classmates, even though Poppy came to school some days and sat in the classroom on an invisible chair. When asked why she had not informed her fellow pupils, she answered, 'Well, other children would say, "That's not true."' Like Bill the engineer who had a fascination with alien abductions, Caitlin chose her audience carefully.

In another group, Henry and Marnie, aged eight, were discussing their experiences. Marnie had seen a glittering light outside her bedroom window which she thought was a fairy. She went to brush her teeth and then returned to the window to see if the light was still there, which it was. She got into bed, then turned off her light and crept out of bed again to take another look, but it had disappeared. When I asked if she had told anyone she said that she had told her mum, who just replied that it must have been her imagination, which seemed to have disappointed her. Fortunately she felt comfortable enough in our group to share her experience. Henry told us about a white ghost which had been looking at him through a window and explained that he had not told anybody because 'they'll just think that's not true'.

Needing to belong

Children's need to feel that they belong to their peer group can lead them to adapt their behaviour so that it conforms to their group's norms. Whilst such behaviours are usually thought of in terms of style of dress, music and social activities, the behaviours also relate to topics of conversation including what is acceptable to discuss. In societies where value is seemingly placed on the material and not on the inner or the imaginative, children are more likely to keep these aspects of their life hidden unless they can find an empathic listener.

When children feel misunderstood on a regular basis, this can have damaging consequences for their self-esteem and exacerbate feelings of loneliness. Whilst feeling misunderstood occurs in many different areas of a child's life, and is indeed inevitable at times, as it is in adulthood too, this scenario is particularly sensitive when relating to unseen worlds. Through experiencing these lands and the beings that inhabit them, children construct their understanding of their own place in the world. For many who have invisible companions, it is mystifying that no one else can see them. For these children who do not understand their companion to be a *pretend* playmate, how can they make sense of their invisible friend's existence when other people are saying they exist purely in their minds? Whilst children have significant capacities to make sense of different aspects of life, if they consistently feel that no one understands what they are experiencing, they may begin to doubt their own mind and suppress their experiences.

Some recommendations

- It is easy to assume that because children are increasingly visible in our society, and have the legal right to be heard, they will naturally voice their experiences of unseen worlds. However, in order to do so they will need to feel that they will be taken seriously. Adults need to ensure that children in their care will receive appropriate, supportive responses which indicate a genuine interest in what they have to say.

- Be sensitive about the pressures older children feel to disassociate themselves with young children and align themselves with older children. Children are developing their identity and may be struggling to reconcile their experiences with the growing awareness that others deem them 'childish'.

- Although adults use the phrase 'it's just your imagination' in order to comfort or reassure children who are unsettled or frightened by an experience, this can be a potentially damaging phrase. Instead, try to explore the child's feelings with them or offer a sympathetic ear. (Unless adults are qualified counsellors, other professionals should not feel pressurised to act in a therapeutic role.)

- As children grow older they are increasingly aware of the meaning of the word 'imagination'. It is interesting to enter into dialogue with children who are discussing an experience which many would label imagination, because they can offer interesting insights into why they do not share the 'it's just your imagination' theory in some instances. Their explanations are often very much rooted in rational thinking, as a conversation with eight-year-olds about Santa Claus' arrival at their house with presents demonstrated.

'You know the Santa Claus thing…' said Marnie.

Henry interrupted 'Every Christmas Eve I put out a glass of sherry and carrots and they are always gone…'

'The only reason probably why they put out sherry is because the adults drink it,' Marnie laughed.

'No, my Mum's on a diet! …and I can hear her snoring, because her bedroom is next to mine so I hear her snoring,' explained Henry.

Henry was aware that others did not believe in Santa but his defence of him was very much based on logic. By talking to children, rather than simply closing a conversation by referring to imagination, significant insights can be made into their worldviews as well as offering affirmation.

- Contemplate responses carefully and be aware of your body language which might indicate a lack of interest. If the child approaches you in a busy period, explain that you would really like to hear their experiences later on. If possible, agree when that will be and follow through, so that the child feels that you value what they have to say.

Children need to have a respectful and interested ear if they desire to share and explore their experiences with others. Adults have a key role to play in providing this supportive role, whether or not they deem the accounts to be 'just imagination'. However, barriers to accepting children's worlds are numerous and go beyond simply holding a different viewpoint, which the following chapter explores in more depth.

CHAPTER 7

Accepting children's worlds

A colleague asked me what my book was about. After offering a synopsis, she paused for a moment before saying, 'Mmm, that sounds interesting. Children have such vivid imaginations don't they?' and we continued our conversation. Like many others, she accepted the children's worlds which I described to her in the sense that they are a part of what she and our culture associate with childhood. But her acceptance remained only at that superficial level, i.e. children play, imagine and create both wonderful and frightening worlds in their minds; that is what children do. If there is a spectrum of acceptance, then she would be placed at the beginning of it. She seemed reluctant to consider acceptance on a deeper level, not necessarily to believe that fairies, imaginary companions and ghosts 'exist', but to acknowledge that these are 'real' to the children in the sense that adults define 'real'. As adults we need to understand that, for many children, these worlds have a considerable impact on their sense of self and their place in the world.

The previous chapter considered the range of responses that adults give to children when they express their encounters with unseen worlds and how those reactions might affect the children. It was proposed that some of the barriers to effective responses include adults' lack of time and their conceptions of what might constitute 'childish' behaviour. This chapter undertakes a deeper exploration of adults' barriers to a more complete acceptance, before revisiting affirming ways of responding to children's experiences in the next chapter.

Self reflection

A key characteristic required by practitioners engaging with children is a skill to be self-reflective, as indicated in chapter 1. For those who have undertaken professional training it is likely that the concept of the reflective practitioner has been covered. For example in order to meet the standards for Qualified Teacher Status in England, student teachers are required to 'reflect on and improve their practice' as well as encourage pupils to reflect on their own learning (TDA 2008, p. 6). The principles of self-reflection in professional contexts tend to relate to being aware of one's practice; being mindful of how it is purposeful, constructive and achieves its outcomes in addition to identifying the weaknesses of practice and how they can be improved.

The notion of the reflective practitioner has been influenced by the works of Dewey (1933) and more recently Schön (1983). Dewey (1933) made a distinction between routine action and reflective action, with the former being shaped by traditional behaviours and routine habit which rarely changes. In comparison, an individual engaging in reflective action is motivated to develop themselves and regularly self-appraise. Schön (1983) used the terms knowing-in-action and reflecting-in-action. The former refers to actions and judgements which are learnt and made spontaneously, often being done automatically. In contrast, reflecting-in-action occurs when an individual thinks consciously about the activity whilst it is being undertaken. Through reflection, adults can increase their self knowledge and understand the reasons for their actions at a deeper level, thereby allowing them to refine and improve their practice.

In relation to children's worlds, the principles of self-reflection apply to adults on a variety of levels. First, they apply to adults identifying their own perspectives by becoming aware of their attitudes towards them; second, to becoming conscious of the origins of those views; third, being cognisant of alternative perspectives; fourth, examining their ideas of the distinction between fantasy and reality; and finally being mindful of how their responses to children are conveyed and received. This chapter examines the first four points, with the fifth being explored in chapter 8.

Identifying one's own perspectives

The first step for adults in accepting children's worlds beyond the fact that they are a part of childhood is to clarify their own perspectives on each of the various phenomena. Robert, in his fifties, commented,

> Well, I'm pretty open to the idea that ghosts exist. After all, we certainly don't understand everything about the world and there are so many mysterious things which happen to people that we can't explain. I've had one or two weird encounters myself. As for fairies, I see those as an important part of mythology which is reinforced in children's books but no, I don't think I would say they existed. Imaginary friends are a bit more difficult because I'm tempted to say that children probably create them for a bit of company, but on the other hand my niece sits and chats away to someone for hours at a time which I find quite intriguing.

Whilst Robert does not believe that fairies exist, this is not a barrier to him accepting the reality of them for children. An open-minded response such as 'whilst I do not personally believe in that, I can see why another person does' is a sound basis for developing understanding with children.

Becoming conscious of one's attitudes towards unseen worlds is essential because they can affect how adults respond to children. Adults may, of course, have different views about different aspects of the worlds, perhaps believing in ghosts because they have seen or sensed one, but being sceptical about imaginary companions, assuming them to be playful creations of lonely children. Adults' dispositions will also vary, with some responding affectionately but superficially towards children's accounts and others taking a more enquiring, in-depth approach.

Further, these responses may again differ according to the matter which is being discussed. For example, if the child is claiming to have heard sleigh bells and seen Santa Claus sneaking into their bedroom with a sack of presents, adults will undoubtedly react with an encouraging smile or comment so as not to dent their enthusiasm. When a child is describing having seen a deceased relative, the response will be less superficial because the event raises more substantive issues surrounding grief and loss and the possibilities of an afterlife. Once practitioners have reflected on their personal positions, they will be better prepared to respond to children with integrity.

The origins of worldviews and the impact of culture

However, simply being aware of one's stance(s) is not sufficient alone; it is also important for adults to understand their own reasons for adopting their respective beliefs about unseen worlds as this skill will facilitate empathy with children even when their respective beliefs or experiences differ. The origins of adults' views lie in part in their upbringing, as shaped by their culture, and it is essential to be mindful of these origins which can easily be taken for granted. Religion provides a good example. Whilst a small proportion of adults convert to a different faith, the vast majority of religious adults retain the affiliation to the belief system in which they were raised. Certainly, many may have questioned their faith at some point or points in their life, but there is no denying the influence of the particular religion in which their parents/carers nurtured them, i.e. the religion that was determined by their immediate culture.

Studies in different cultures clearly show how experiences, vocabulary and beliefs differ, as the following example illustrates. Coles (1992, pp.152–153) talked to Natalie, an eight-year-old girl from the Hopi community in North America who explained her beliefs about how the spirits of her ancestors lived in the mesa and how the wind helped them travel between there and the earth. The ancestors whispered to the elders of the community who then passed on their wisdom to the younger people. Natalie would sit near a window and pray to her ancestors, asking them to include her. She explained,

> My thoughts cross our land and they are heard on the mesa. They are like the birds. They rise and circle and circle, and then they gradually head for the mesa, and our ancestors wait there for news of us. Then I hear news of them.

Neither Natalie nor her family were comfortable with the word 'God', instead preferring the word 'spirit', as in the collective spirit of the Hopi ancestors and their own spirits. Natalie's account is clearly rooted in her own cultural beliefs, as her language conveys and is easily distinguishable from Western children's descriptions of spirits.

Another area of disparity across different cultures is that of the near-death experience. In chapter 3, a common understanding of an NDE was described as being close to death and being pulled through a long dark space where a person can encounter deep feelings of peace and glimpse into another world where deceased relatives or friends may be waiting. Whilst this portrayal will be familiar, Kellehear (1996) emphasises that it is only a popular image because it is in fact a classical Western image. Reports from other countries, although having basic similar features, have their own distinguishing characteristics. For example, people in Melanesia tend to see villages; in a study of 45 cases in India, there was no evidence of a tunnel sensation and only one case of an out-of-body experience. In Guam, experients report flying through the clouds and seeing a place of garden-like appearance where they are met by deceased people (Kellehear 1996). In the case of children reporting what appear to be previous lives, Stevenson (1987) also points out differences in cases across cultures. One such example is found in cases of children remembering a previous life in which they were part of the same family. This feature was present in the majority of reports from Burma and Thailand but was far less frequent in India, Lebanon and Sri Lanka. Further, in Lebanon, Turkey and the Tlingit communities of Alaska, the gender of the previous reincarnation was always the same as the informant's present gender but in Burma this was not the case, with 28 per cent of the accounts referring to being of the opposite sex in the past-life.

Whilst such differences in culture can be quite stark, cultural influences also impact on belief systems in more subtle ways. In the West, where information is increasingly available and children are exposed to an ever-growing body of knowledge, children have access to more ideas and images than has ever been possible, or conceivable, in the past. As globalisation increases, children not only encounter different ideas through the media but also through direct contact with friends and classmates from a variety of cultural backgrounds. Concurrently, education systems recognise the importance of learning about historical traditions, myths and life in different cultures, with some curricula also teaching about world religions and other belief systems. Children thus accumulate and assimilate ideas from a range of cultures both present and historic, both consciously and subconsciously. Whilst the culture of their parents and immediate community may predominate, children also co-construct their reality; influences from many areas of life such as television, friends and lessons in school can shape their belief systems.

In a liberal society which is home to a wide range of different cultures, religions and secular influences, various ideas thus weave together. Hyde (2008) explored children's spirituality in Catholic primary schools in Australia where he found that many drew not simply on their Catholic upbringing but also on other religious and philosophical ideas in order to understand events in their life. Even children who were not from religious homes drew on different belief systems in their search for meaning. Hyde retells the story of Jake who was describing the recent death of his dog Scamper. Jake explained that a neighbour's dog gave birth to puppies around the time of Scamper's death. 'I think that maybe Scamper's spirit is sort of alive in one of those baby pups... One of them even looks a bit like Scamper...' Jake's ideas resemble a form of reincarnation which he appears to have gleaned from a television programme. By drawing on eclectic ideas Jake, like many children, is able to make sense of his experiences (Hyde 2008, p.14). Many adults, when confronted with children's experiences inevitably respond by drawing on their own cultural upbringing, either consciously or unconsciously. However, the degree of accuracy of information offered can be variable as there can be a tendency to rely on one's own personal experience in conversations.

In the current digital age, information is everywhere. With a click of a button a person can access almost any information they want (not that it is necessarily reliable); books and leaflets can be accessed for free in libraries or downloaded; there are magazines offering explicit advice about almost any subject; and a range of seemingly endless digital and satellite television channels fill our minds with details about anything in which we are interested. In theory, then, people should be knowledgeable about a wide range of issues and in comparison to previous centuries this is certainly the case. However, the human brain can only assimilate so much information and in order to survive the demands of modern life, adults need to focus on that which is required for their daily routine, whether it be how to care for the needs of a baby, or how to function effectively in a voluntary or paid role. Leisure time offers opportunities for seeking out more information on topics or issues of personal interest but the amount of information available on any topic can be overwhelming. Magazines and television programmes offer bite-size chunks that are tailor-made for busy lifestyles but cannot offer in-depth knowledge and lack of time can inhibit a person from seeking out more detailed and critical views on a given topic. Inevitably, people often revert to opinions and personal experiences rather than findings based in research (research findings in themselves can be contradictory of course!) when they offer explanations for matters such as those encountered in children's worlds.

People's attitudes towards dreams are good examples of this phenomenon of relying on our own experience to explain a situation because, aside from a small percentage of people who cannot remember their dreams, all people dream and the vast majority have some recall of them, no matter how fleeting. Dreams have fascinated humankind since time began (Van de Castle 1994) and, as detailed below, cultures provide different frameworks for understanding their causes and functions. For now, remaining with a Western perspective, imagine the following scenario.

DREAMING OF ALIENS

> Joe, a six-year-old boy, reports dreaming that he was on another planet playing games with some furry alien creatures. He maintains that the aliens were friendly and had promised he could visit them again next week. Joe insists that he really had travelled to their land and hadn't just dreamt it. His mother is touched by his account and narrates it to her husband later that day, commenting 'He dreamt about that because of the film we enjoyed watching yesterday which had furry aliens in it, he thought they were really cute.'

The boy's mother is naturally drawing on her own experience of dreaming which is usually linked to our experiences of the day. As noted in chapter 4, Freud (1900) used the term 'day residue' to indicate the material of the waking hours which reappears during dreams. Further, fictional characters from the media are present in many contemporary dream reports. Such findings are hardly surprising, yet there are other perspectives to consider in addition to the fact that images, experiences and emotions from daily life shape dream content. For example, a psychoanalytic approach would suggest that dreams embody messages from the subconscious. Such a theory would pose the question as to why the aliens appeared in Joe's dream rather than any other characters from the film. Further, given all of the thoughts, feelings, sensations and experiences of the day, the film occupied a relatively small amount, so why did the dream select the film in particular?

Joe's dream is also quite characteristic of his personality. He is a friendly, sociable boy and this personality trait is shown in the dream where he is enjoying himself playing with others. This aspect concurs with the continuity hypothesis of dreaming, which holds that our personality is also reflected in our dreams (Van de Castle 1994, Domhoff 2001). Again, this theory will not be surprising to those who have not heard of it before, but whilst studies have supported it, others have challenged it on the grounds of Jung's theory of the compensatory function of dreaming. This theory proposes that the psyche needs to achieve balance by developing awareness of parts of a personality that are neglected or suppressed. Dreams can give expression to this hidden part of the personality, thereby providing an alternative viewpoint to the continuity hypothesis theory.

Yet such rationalist theories are not the only ones to consider because some cultures perceive dreams to be ventures of the soul into other lands. For example, Lohmann (2001) spent time living with the Asabano tribe of Papua New Guinea and learnt how they understood dreams to be the wanderings of the disembodied soul in which they meet others, including ancestors, and other religious and spiritual beings. The dream, according to this way of thinking, is literally a journey into other worlds which lies in stark contrast to the notion of a dream being a collection of images and noises produced by randomly firing neurons in the brain, which is the dominant conception in neuroscience. In this case, Joe certainly had a sense of having been in another place and had he been a member of a community which believed dreams to be a journey of the soul, his explanation of it would have been deemed natural.

Finally, Joe's mother is expressing a natural urge to account for the dream's content, which is a common reaction. This desire to rationalise and understand for oneself is often an automatic response and one which is considered further later in this chapter because the process can obstruct understanding the experience from the child's perspective. Overall, whilst Joe's mother is not in the business of interpreting her son's dream, the narrative is told in order to illustrate that there are wider issues involved in understanding what a person dreams about and why. Joe's mother has listened to her son and accepted his dream but only on a superficial level. She is interested and touched by it and accepts it in the sense that it conforms to her understanding of dreams, namely that people's daily experiences often form dream content. She has, quite naturally, placed her own cultural understanding of dreams on Joe's experience. Like most people, she cannot be expected to know what researchers have discovered or hypothesised, but in order to fully understand Joe's encounter, she would benefit from exploring different explanations. In addition, she would have attained greater insight into Joe's perspective by engaging in further conversation with him rather than simply imposing her own explanation on it.

Alternative perspectives

In order to be able to gauge an appropriate response to children's worlds, it is important to reflect not only on one's own views but also on different interpretations of the same event. Such reflection is necessary given the cultural constructions of various unseen worlds. It is vital that we understand that our own outlook is at least in part derived from our own cultural upbringing or experience, and a person may be limiting themselves if they do not consider wider perspectives. This argument can be exemplified with two cases, one of Daniel who sees his deceased grandmother and the other of Jasmine who suffers from a recurring nightmare.

DANIEL'S GRANDMOTHER

Daniel, aged eight, mentioned to his father that he regularly saw his grandmother sitting in a chair in the corner of the living room. Daniel did not question seeing her and had simply assumed that his parents could also see her. To him, his grandmother was simply *there*.

How can Daniel's world, inhabited by his deceased grandmother be explained? From a psychological perspective, Daniel's experience is an anticipated part of the grieving process. Psychologists have identified a series of (often non-linear) stages which people progress through following bereavement including shock or denial of the death which is often accompanied by feelings of numbness. During this phase, people often report seeing the deceased person in the course of daily life. Fear, anger, guilt, relief and a sense of searching for the deceased can follow in a period of disorganisation. When the bereaved is able to reorganise, they can begin to accept the loss, adjust to it and begin to reinvest in life (Garfield 1996). Daniel's experience of seeing his grandmother can thus be explained in psychological terms in relation to the grieving process.

Religious interpretations also offer another possible explanation. A characteristic of religious beliefs throughout the world, is the concept that life continues after the body's physical death in some form. Hinduism, for example, embodies the belief in Samsara, the endless cycle of birth and rebirth through which souls go. Traditional Christianity sees a judgement on a soul being made at death which indicates whether it is destined for heaven or hell. In the Cherokee and Iroquois cultures of North America, souls may be required to pass a test before they are permitted to enter the land of the dead (Hinnells 1997).

The Christian Spiritualist church, although a relatively minor religious movement in most Western countries, has churches in many towns and cities. Their faith centres upon the belief that communication with the spirits of deceased people is accessible through a medium – a person who is able to receive messages from spirits either directly or through a spirit guide. During a typical service, following prayers and hymns, a medium delivers greetings and personal messages from deceased relatives and friends to members of the congregation (Hinnells 1997). According to this worldview, Daniel may have been seeing the spirit of his grandmother.

In secular terminology, which is also used by many children in daily discourse, Daniel's vision of his grandmother as seen in the armchair, might be referred to as a ghost. Whilst children's media often depicts ghosts as resembling a white sheet floating around, other media portrays them as the spirits of people or animals who have died. These can range from an historical character roaming the corridors of a castle whilst holding his head to a loving grandmother baking cakes. Children will naturally absorb the variety of images they see on screen or in books and develop their own conceptions of what a ghost is like.

Finally, Daniel's experience can of course be classified as 'just his imagination'. Undoubtedly his grandmother would have been occupying his thoughts and a possible subconscious desire to see her again might have manifested itself in her apparent appearance. Alternatively, her presence – perhaps influenced by Daniel's wishes – may have been a trick of the light.

These various explanations are all possibilities and none can be proven. Each alternative is largely dependent upon a belief or worldview and because of this it is important for adults to reflect on explanations which are different from their own. An adult who is convinced that the notion of spirits is pure fantasy is likely to impose that worldview on a child's claim of seeing one, i.e. that it was just imagination. Similarly an adult who believes that Daniel has seen his grandmother's spirit may convey this to him (depending on the context of their setting). All explanations are equally valid but do need to take into account Daniel's view as well.

A second exemplification of the argument to examine perspectives from outside one's own framework is offered with the case of Jasmine's recurring nightmare.

JASMINE'S NIGHTMARE

> Jasmine, aged seven, would regularly awake in the night screaming in terror. She told her mother that a large, scaly creature climbed onto her bed and sat on top of her. As the creature was about to bite her, she awoke but could not move, panicked that there was no escape.

How can Jasmine's encounter with a monster in the night be explained? In the West, her experience will be often automatically classified as a nightmare, which is a normal part of childhood (Woolley and Wellman 1992, Hartmann 1996, Siegel and Bulkeley 1998, Mallon 2002). However, the term 'nightmare' is in part a social construction and different cultures have understood them in different ways. For example, ancient Egyptians believed that the spirits of citizens of the underworld caused nightmares (Szpakowska 2001). Indeed, the concept that nightmares are produced by external forces such as demons, witches, ghosts of the deceased or tribal enemies was a key belief in many cultures prior to the twentieth century (Siegel and Bulkeley 1998).

As mentioned briefly in chapter 5, Siegel and Bulkeley (1998) suggest that nightmares play a role in coping with changes in life, such as beginning school, moving house or parents' divorce. The authors also suggest that the nightmares provide messages that warn the individual to pay attention to situations which threaten their emotional security.

So, Jasmine, like most children, is experiencing a frightening world through a nightmare. Or is she? Another element to Jasmine's experience is her temporary inability to move, suggesting in contemporary psychological terms, that it is a case of sleep paralysis, which is technically different to a nightmare, although equally frightening. In a typical case, the experience occurs during rapid eye movement sleep. The sufferer awakes and hears and/or sees a presence in the room and is temporarily unable to move or cry out, often feeling terror and physical sensations such as being pressed on the chest, or strangled (Parker and Blackmore 2002, Hufford 2005).

As noted above, the influence of culture upon shaping the experience and the understanding of it is significant and sleep paralysis is no exception. Parker and Blackmore (2002) note that there are consistent features in sleep paralysis reports from across the world but that culture plays a role in how it is labelled. For example, in Newfoundland, the person who is paralysed is believed to have been visited by the 'Old Hag' and in Southeast Asia the being is known as the sitting ghost (Hufford 2005). Researchers have noted that sleep paralysis has been implicated in supernatural events and alien abductions (Parker and Blackmore 2002).

Daniel and Jasmine's cases demonstrate that different interpretations of experiences are possible, thereby highlighting the subjective nature of them. For all of the unseen worlds described in this book, there are various ways of making sense of them. For example, different explanations have been offered to account for near-death experiences. It has been argued that they are: evidence for life after death; an imaginative response to the need to deny that death is the end of life; medical phenomena; or are simply hallucinations (Kellehear 1996). It is therefore important that adults consider alternative ways of understanding children's experiences particularly given that various theories have been proposed to explain each and every one, with no definitive consensus having been achieved and many explanations simply resting on personal belief. It is wise not to simply rely on our own experiences or views, but to be aware of alternative perspectives which exist as these can open our own minds to how the children may be making sense of their encounters.

For children particularly, it is not always a straightforward case of them believing in what they have been 'taught'. They are likely to create a framework for understanding which is drawn on a wide variety of ideas gathered from a vast array of sources and adults need to be mindful of this and not assume that a child will restrict themselves to a belief system in which they have been brought up.

'But is it real?' Conceptions of fantasy and reality

A fourth aspect requiring reflection relates to a distinction between fantasy and reality because one of the barriers to being fully open to the realness of children's worlds from their view is a tendency to ask '*but is it real?*' This question often forms part of the process of rationalisation that occurs when searching for explanations to mysterious phenomena. Developmental studies have shown that the majority of children aged from three to eight believe that many fantastical figures and processes, such as magic, ghosts, monsters and the tooth fairy are real rather than being creations of pretend play (Principe and Smith 2007, 2008); but adults often seek to ask whether such worlds are objectively real as opposed to children believing that they are real. We have already seen that cultural constructions can significantly influence a person's understanding of an experience, and this section moves on to examine the question of 'objective reality' from the perspective of psychological literature on children's understanding of reality versus fantasy, using the theme of imaginary companions as a vehicle.

A closer exploration of the concepts of fantasy and reality is required in order to gain an understanding of the research findings which have examined them, primarily drawn from developmental psychology. In everyday language, the two terms are at first glance quite distinct, with the term 'reality' pertaining to that which is physically verifiable whilst 'fantasy' relates to that which is of the mind, fictional or imaginary. Woolley (1997), in her discussion of children's and adults' thinking about fantasy, suggests that there is a continuum of commitment to what people think the world is like. At one end are the things people describe as real, which are entities and processes that concur with their theories of the world which are supported by empirical evidence. At the opposite end are those to which no commitment is made, for example the fantasy-type thinking in which people engage when reading a novel. In between each end of the spectrum, she suggests, are a number of different beliefs which can vary according to each individual. Towards the end of the continuum marked 'real' are those things for which a person does not have sufficient empirical evidence to definitively mark them as real. For Woolley, an example is the notion that UFOs containing aliens from other planets have visited the Earth. She considers this to be a possibility but feels that she has not yet seen sufficient evidence to substantiate the claim that aliens have landed. Finally, towards the 'unreal' end of the continuum are beliefs which may threaten an individual's theories but to which some commitment may be made, for example superstitious or magical beliefs. This phenomenon is evidenced in an adult who understands the physical laws of cause and effect but nevertheless avoids walking under a ladder in case it brings them bad luck.

Early researchers such as Piaget thought that children tended to confuse fantasy and reality, but as Woolley (1997), Sharon and Woolley (2004) and Principe and Smith (2008) all observe, there is an increasing body of literature which shows that even young children can readily differentiate between them. These claims are based on a wide number of psychological experiments which have given children different tasks to complete. An example may be to ask children to imagine that there is a pink rabbit sitting inside a box. Here, the children know that there is no pink rabbit and that it exists only in their imagination. Principe and Smith (2008) do, however, urge caution that this ability to distinguish between fantasy and reality is sometimes fragile, particularly when children are asked to imagine events and later report whether or not the events took place. In some cases children appeared to confuse imagined events with real events in memory, even when adults had explained that the events had not actually occurred.

Woolley (1997) suggests that when children engage in magical thinking it is not because they are confused about the reality–fantasy distinction, but is in fact linked to their knowledge of mental and physical phenomena. A child may thus know that thinking about an event cannot make it happen, but they appeal to their knowledge of magic to propose that *magic* can make something happen, via them wishing for it. Bouldin and Pratt (2001) propose a similar argument, drawing on the work of Subbotsky (1984) who suggests that children hold to belief systems which are distinct from each other and inconsistent. These are first, that everyday beliefs differentiate between fantasy and reality and second, that other beliefs allow for extraordinary, magical happenings. This hypothesis is highly credible as it is equally applicable to adults who can distinguish between fantasy and reality yet simultaneously believe in supernatural events.

The hypotheses and conclusions of these psychological studies on the reality–fantasy distinction are important for stimulating debate amongst adults seeking to understand how children perceive reality and fantasy, particularly because researchers do not necessarily concur with each other. However, a philosophical issue is certainly raised about the meaning of the words reality and fantasy as it can be argued that researchers are working from a Western standpoint when separating the two.

Are imaginary companions real?

The question about the objective reality of unseen entities is particularly pertinent when discussing imaginary companions with those adults who insist that they are figments of children's imagination which do not deserve particular attention. Such a view – that the companions exist purely in the child's mind – can be in conflict with some children's conviction that the companion is as real as you or me. There is no question that for many children the companions are something they have knowingly created, but for others the companions are very real and this finding led Hallowell (2007, p.7), to not only challenge the phrase 'imaginary friend' as detailed in chapter 5, but also to reject the word 'imaginary'. Instead he replaces it with the term 'quasi-corporeal' because, he argues, these entities are very real to the experients. The children who have them can see and hear them as they would see and hear everyone else around them.

It is important to be aware of researchers' bias and assumptions when they construct and conduct studies with children. For example, Taylor (1999) considers children's imaginary companions to be a form of play and in so doing, her underlying belief appears to be that the companions cannot be 'real' although she values them, perceiving them to be a normal and healthy invention of children's imagination. Hoff (2004, p.180) comes from a similar standpoint which is demonstrated in the wording in her questionnaire to children which asks, 'What do you call your pretend playmate?' Again, Hoff is automatically assuming that the children have created the companions in the course of play. Such views fail to take into account that the companions might be very real to some children. Indeed, Hoff's questionnaire uses the phrase 'pretend playmate' throughout, which also means that her data collection methods would not allow children to express any beliefs they might have about the actual existence of their companions. Hence, her findings may be limited by the restrictive nature of her underlying personal beliefs about imaginary companions. A particular consideration when understanding children's viewpoints lies in the contradictory messages which society gives to them.

Culture – simultaneously supporting and denying unseen worlds?

In some cases, Western culture actively encourages children's belief in unseen worlds especially in their younger years but not simply in the realm of fantasy play. For example, Principe and Smith (2007) argue that many families endorse children's belief in their fantasies by carrying out 'rituals' such as making a wish when blowing out candles on a birthday cake, or crossing fingers for good luck. Further, many parents/carers actively create apparent 'evidence' to support the belief in selected fantasy beings, such as leaving food out for Santa Claus' reindeer or providing carrots for the Easter bunny. Principe and Smith (2007) make a particularly interesting point that many children's fantasies are presented alongside a strong demand to believe in them, for example when saying that there will be no Christmas presents for disbelievers.

'Fantasy characters' such as Santa Claus, the Easter bunny or the tooth fairy are of course, as Principe and Smith (2008) note, myths which adults present to children in a ready-made form. Consequently these characters are in some ways different to most of those detailed in this book as they are not only clearly manufactured by adults but are also given to children alongside fabricated evidence of their existence. Adults further enforce the reality of these figures through books, television programmes and other media.

The presentation of ready-made characters occupies an interesting position compared to other types of entities encountered. In other cases, it can also be argued that ghosts, imaginary companions and monsters are also presented to children in the sense that they appear in books or in digital media and are thus placed in the children's psyche. The difference lies perhaps in the active encouragement of children to believe in not just the figures of Santa Claus or the tooth fairy, but to believe in the 'whole package' as it is stage managed. In contrast, only a minority of parents will seriously encourage children to believe in imaginary companions or in monsters who lurk in the shadows of the bedroom.

Western culture thus seems to present contradictory messages to children; whilst it is active in encouraging fantasy play and beliefs this is perhaps only when the adults can gain some control over it. The creation of Santa Claus is a carefully manufactured affair which is embedded in many cultures in one form or another. It is safe and brings awe and wonder, happiness and excitement to children and teaches them the values of generosity and kindness. There is, however, controversy associated with this myth which Papatheodorou and Gill (2002) explore. They observe how criticisms of the concept relate to how the story introduces deception and lying to children, and the way in which it is over-commercialised.

When adults 'lose control' of the unseen phenomena, that is, when children appear to be the initiators of an experience – perhaps, having claimed to have seen a ghost or having an imaginary companion rather than seeing the tooth fairy leaving some money – then a difference in attitude can become apparent. Rather than affirming the experience of seeing the tooth fairy, the assertion of the ghost or imaginary companion is often dismissed or disregarded. Reasons for this may be manifold, such as not knowing how to respond, not wishing to confront the possibility that such entities might exist or that the child believes in them, or not wanting to contradict something which the child's family might have told them. However, the lack of control over these other, non-manufactured beings may possibly play a role in shaping many adults' responses, not to mention creating confusion for children who on the one hand are told that some beings are real whilst others are products of their imagination.

Barriers to empathy

Cultural barriers to empathising can thus be significant particularly because people often operate without consciously acknowledging those influences as they have become internalised. Morse and Perry (1990) note how medical training in the US at their time of writing did not encourage doctors to talk about death even when working with patients who were terminally ill. One of the consequences, they argue, is that many medical practitioners disregarded accounts of near-death experiences. Their immediate culture – of medical training – effectively created a taboo around conversations about death and ultimately some doctors deemed patients who reported NDEs to be suffering from mental illnesses.

Children are naturally perceptive when it comes to learning which topics are acceptable to discuss in their communities. The unseen worlds that are generally invisible to the wider population, as discussed in chapter 3, are particularly difficult for children to openly discuss with many adults for different reasons, especially the lack of empathy which many adults have.

When we think back to our own childhood, and the ways in which we might have seen things that other people did not see, it is easy to understand how many find it difficult to empathise with children's unseen worlds. An additional and significant barrier to this understanding lies with the fact that children assume that what they see is what everybody else sees; that is until they discover otherwise. Scott (2004) demonstrates this perfectly with his example of Nora, a woman who, as a four- and five-year-old child, could see auras around other people. She thought nothing of this, assuming it was natural, and that everyone saw these colours. One day she mentioned them to her friends and was surprised to learn that they could not see them. She explained, 'I was seeing something they could not see. I never saw lights around people again until I was in my 30s' (p.71).

Nora's situation provides a good example of how society affects children's perception of the unseen. Children have no reason to assume that other people experience the world differently. For example, a child who is colourblind will assume that others see the grass as being the same colour as they see it until they learn otherwise, perhaps when they reach for a different coloured pencil when drawing a picture of grass. It is often only through experience or through talking about what we see, feel or sense that we begin to understand that others do not experience the world in the same way. For Nora, her realisation came when she told her friends about the auras, but that conversation had a profound effect by preventing her from seeing them for the next two decades.

Another barrier to empathy lies in the tendency to disassociate with our own childhoods, partly due to the effect of adult filters through which we come to see our childhood. Again this process is not necessarily intentional (unless of course an individual is consciously trying to block out traumatic events). The passing of time and gaining of life experience can make it difficult to associate with the small person we were as seen in photographs taken during our first few years. Simon, a computer technician, remembered playing a card game with his friend Nathan when they were eleven. Nathan was dealing the cards when Simon realised that he could predict what each card was going to be as if he could 'see through' them. Suddenly Nathan appeared to acquire this skill and knew what the next card was going to be. Neither of the boys could explain this unusual occurrence, which had never happened before and never happened since. Over twenty years on, Simon's astonishment at this temporary supernatural ability had distinctly subsided and he surmised that the only explanation was that the cards had been in the same order as the previous dealing, which the boys had unwittingly memorised. I asked Simon if he could recall any other experiences and he remembered seeing a ghost in the hallway of his grandmother's house. 'I was on holiday there with my family and there was a blue urn in the hallway and I distinctly remember seeing a ghost next to it which was something of a shock! However, I realise now that I only saw it because we had been watching Doctor Who on the television.' Simon has become slightly distanced from his childhood experiences. He acknowledges that at the time, the pre-cognitive skill and the ghostly sighting made a considerable impact on him. However, with passing decades the impact has waned and he now favours more rational explanations for these events which he could not explain in his youth.

Our personalities naturally have some bearing on how we respond to such experiences, both as a child and as an adult. Simon now describes himself as a 'down-to-earth and grounded' man, which is reflected in his current thoughts. In contrast, Bernard, the social worker referred to in chapter 2, still retains some sense of mystery about his childhood experiences. Bernard described a night spent at his friend's house as a young teenager.

> Mick and I were sleeping in adjacent rooms separated by a landing. In the early hours of the morning I heard a bang which woke me up. There was some light coming through the window and I clearly saw a man hunched over the bedroom door holding the handle. I was so terrified I closed my eyes and then Mick screamed 'Did you see it?!' As incredible as it sounds we both saw this man at the same time. I am still troubled by it and although it seems as if we both had a shared hallucination, to be honest, I can't really explain it to this day.

In a separate incident Bernard accompanied his parents and siblings on a house-hunting expedition when he was four or five years old. They visited a three-storey Victorian house which had a long narrow corridor leading down to the kitchen. On the right-hand side of the wall Bernard saw three large arches and a typing pool on the other side. He thought no more of it until the family moved into the house a few months later. Bernard was surprised to find that the arches and the office were no longer there. Today Bernard has no explanation for what he saw. The house, which was part of a terrace, had only ever been used as housing and never for business purposes and the wall where he saw the arches had always been a solid wall that separated it from the house next door. This rendered any potential supernatural or parapsychological explanation somewhat unlikely. Bernard retains an open mind about both experiences.

Accepting children's unseen worlds

Simon and Bernard, by virtue of their experiences and different ways of thinking, are likely to respond to children's worlds in different ways. Simon is more likely to take a pragmatic view, mentally assigning a rational explanation to a child's encounter, even if he does not express it verbally whilst Bernard may be more amenable to alternative explanations. There is no right or wrong in these two approaches. Accepting children's unseen worlds does not mean that adults have to believe in something contrary to their own worldview. Simon now has a daughter who tells him that she has a guardian angel who sits on her bed each night as she falls asleep. Simon does not believe in angels, but neither does he have to in order to validate his daughter's narratives. Instead, he can accept that his daughter believes that she sees the angel. The need to see the worlds through their eyes is vital, but this ability does not necessitate compromising one's own views.

Some recommendations

- An important step on the journey to accepting children's worlds is to reflect on their own views and clarify them because this will enable more sincere communication with children. It is important to understand where your own beliefs have originated and how they have developed.

- Always be cognisant of, and open to, different explanations for children's experiences, including those which emanate from different cultures. There is always more than one possible explanation for encounters with unseen worlds and the child's view is as valid as many others as they continually search to make meaning of life and find their own place in the world. Accepting children's worlds should not just be based on your own cultural beliefs. Be alert to other worldviews; unseen worlds are very much a 'grey' area, requiring an open mind and are inherently subjective in their nature.

- Whilst it is natural for adults to try to offer an explanation for an event, especially if the child has been distressed by it, there are times when explanations are not required by the child. Sometimes, all they need is a listening ear.

- Reflecting on our own personality traits is essential because they will affect how we respond to children's narratives, both inwardly and outwardly.

- Be aware that even if a child is from a religious home, they may nevertheless draw on an eclectic range of ideas and belief systems when making sense of their worlds; do not make assumptions about a child's view based on what you know about their upbringing.

- In order to accept children's unseen worlds, you do not have to compromise your own beliefs. Rather, accept the children's beliefs just as a practising Christian may accept the views of an atheist or a Hindu without adopting their stance.

- Recognise that adults often give children mixed messages about what is real and what is fantasy, according to their own cultural context. One day adults are telling children that Santa Claus will magically fly around the world with presents for all well-behaved children and the next they are dismissive of magical characters such as elves. Confusion for children is often created by adults, and children will inevitably start to ask questions about the 'manufactured' events. Whilst these are questions to be answered in the home and not in a professional setting, be aware that children receive contradictory messages about the unseen.

When an individual can accept children's worlds as being meaningful to the children, whether or not it resonates with their own experience, the greater the opportunities are to affirm them with sincerity. The following chapter considers this concept of affirmation in more detail, offering practical advice for doing so in a variety of settings.

CHAPTER 8

Affirming children's worlds

Accepting the notion of children's worlds as being meaningful or significant to children is not always a straightforward matter for every practitioner, but once the concept has been accepted in principle, adults need to gain access to the children's experiences and respond to them. As discussed previously, there is a range of responses available, which are often affected by the adult's own experiences, openness, levels of empathy and their opinions on the matter in hand. Given that a negative response can cause a child to retreat into silence, it is essential that adults find ways to affirm their experiences in ways which demonstrate integrity. This chapter explores the implications of the material presented for those interacting with children, discussing the need for practitioners (as well as parents/carers) to access and affirm children's experiences and feelings where appropriate. Practical advice is offered alongside the recognition of the potential difficulties of this process and a focus on dealing with the darker aspects of children's fears.

Accessing children's worlds

As detailed earlier, some of the worlds which children inhabit are more easily accessible to adults than others. Some, such as fantasy, role, symbolic and imaginative play are immediately observable and at times allow adults to actively participate in them. Others, such as dreaming or seeing deceased relatives can remain hidden and depend upon the child communicating the experience. Of course, not all children will choose to share these aspects of their lives. Some will simply want to keep them private whilst others will want to share but are reluctant to do so for fear of dismissal or not being believed. Older children may feel that they will be perceived as being childish and so hide the worlds as they make their transition into the teenage world.

A practitioner or parent/carer's ability to access children's worlds will in part depend on their openness to the concept that for many children, these worlds can be very real. Further, adults' openness to the wide range of worlds and the impact they may have on children is another factor affecting adults' access to them. It may be the case that there are worlds narrated in this book that readers have not necessarily considered before. For example, if children do not share their dream worlds, readers may not have previously given any due attention to children's dreams because it is rarely a topic of serious conversation in daily life. Accessing the worlds can therefore depend in part on being aware of the range of children's possible experiences.

Once individuals are aware, a key factor in gaining further access is by developing relationships with the children which are characterised by trust and mutual respect. Children are highly responsive and open in the company of adults whom they trust to listen carefully, explain where necessary, and above all, be non-judgemental. The concept of being non-judgemental is largely derived from counselling and whilst professionals beyond counselling will not necessarily receive training in this area, it is a highly valuable skill with wide application to all those working with children.

The one-to-one or small group situations in which counsellors may work facilitate a non-judgemental approach not only because of the purpose of the interactions but also because time is built into the situations. For practitioners in other fields where counselling is not the objective, being non-judgemental can be far more challenging because of the competing priorities which they may face. McLaughlin, Carnell and Blount (1999) argue that the principle of being non-judgemental is particularly difficult to transfer to school settings for a variety of reasons. One of the problems, they suggest, is that in schools, children are placed into groups and talking one-to-one with children is quite rare in the hectic and structured timetable of the school day. They also note that part of a teacher's role is to be judgemental as in being required to judge standards of learning/assessment and behaviour.

The nature of relationships between practitioners and children clearly differs from setting to setting. In primary schools, a child usually has a core teacher with whom they spend most of the day, whilst in secondary schools, a pupil will have a variety of teachers and may only see each individual teacher a few times each week. Leaders of faith groups may see a child once a week, social workers may see a child at regular or irregular intervals over different periods of time, whilst healthcare practitioners may see individuals for varying lengths depending on their illness. How open the child is will not necessarily depend upon the amount of time they spend with the adult. As researchers have shown via their findings, children can be very expressive of personal matters when talking to a researcher whom they have never met before and will not meet again, whilst simultaneously stating that they do not share such matters with their parents whom they see every day. Many people, children and adults alike, can find it easier to share personal information with a stranger than with someone they know well. Researchers have an immediate advantage because children are aware that they have an innate interest in what they have to say and will therefore take them seriously. The researcher openly declares their area of interest (via the processes of gaining informed consent from adult gatekeepers and the children themselves) which indicates to children which areas of enquiry the researcher will take seriously.

Access to children's unseen worlds can be more difficult for practitioners who work with children on a daily basis than it might be for researchers. These challenges are not only related to the pressures of time to listen and the nature of group settings in some contexts. A practitioner may have a strong, trusting relationship with the children they work with but it is not necessarily a given that children will automatically share their inner experiences with that adult. After all, children rarely tell researchers that their teachers are confidantes of such information, despite the fact that teachers are the people with whom they spend the most time outside of their home. In order for an adult to be permitted access to a child's worlds, the child needs to be sure that the adult will take them seriously in this particular aspect of their lives. The existence of mutual respect is not always the only necessary condition. A child might, for example, trust an adult enough to tell them they are being bullied or are worried about something yet might be hesitant to reveal an experience of seeing a ghost or having an invisible friend. Why? Children are often very astute when gauging how others might respond to them, and become more selective as they become older, based partly on the responses they have received in the past. It is during childhood that we learn to judge to whom we can and cannot tell certain things. Few adults will tell any one friend everything, as Cheung, an American-Chinese businessman in his 30s, explains.

> I work in a very dynamic and challenging business environment where there is little time to chat during the working day, but some of my colleagues and I socialise every Friday night. They are a great bunch of guys and we get on really well and I know I can trust them not to divulge any of that work-related stuff I confide in them. Yet when I had problems in my marriage, I turned to my friend Josh who, I guess, is pretty much in tune with his feminine side, as you'd say, and is a really good and empathic listener. The guys at work are just too busy putting on a macho front and when I approached one of them about my marital issues, he just laughed it off and said I needed to leave her and find someone younger. I don't believe he meant that seriously, but he just wasn't a good listener, or wasn't ready for that kind of deep conversation. But don't get me wrong, they are all really trustworthy guys.

Like most adults, Cheung has built a network of people around him who have different roles in terms of the types of personal conversations he can have. Whilst young children tend to be very open naturally, by the age of seven or eight they can become more discriminating about what they tell to whom. It is children of this age and above who tell researchers they are worried about being disbelieved or made fun of, often a result of already having told others something personal and having received a negative reaction. This happened to Courtney, aged eight, who told me that she no longer told her father about her 'special' dreams which appeared to tell the future because she told him once and 'he didn't believe me cos he says I was making it up cos it's not possible to know the future before it has happened'.

So, for children to be open about their inner worlds, it is not simply enough that they like and trust the person in question. They also need to be confident in their own minds that the adult they want to tell will be sympathetic to the particular subject matter. Adults thus need to be highly conscious of the messages and signals they convey to the children in their care about such topics because even 'throw away comments' such as 'there is no such thing as ghosts' or 'it's impossible for someone to be invisible' can act as a warning to the child that the adult may not take them seriously. Whilst practitioners may not personally believe in ghosts, most would maintain a professional stance if a child were to ask a direct question: 'Do ghosts exist?' For example they might reply with a question such as, 'What do you think?' or with a statement such as, 'While some people believe in them others don't'. However, messages given outside the context of a direct question can convey the adult's true feelings, which some children will detect. It is thus essential that adults are always mindful of their comments and body language whenever related topics arise, whether it be through children's initiation, reading a story or through a planned activity such as drawing or creative writing.

Children's expressions

The ways in which children's worlds are accessed will naturally depend to some extent on the setting and its individual context. In any situation, children may spontaneously divulge their thoughts, questions and experiences, which is particularly the case for younger children who are more naturally expressive and not yet conscious that adults may disbelieve them. In circumstances where children are required to perform prescribed tasks such as in learning settings or during mental health assessments, the spontaneity may be reduced, but not necessarily eliminated, as children's minds may wander from the task in hand.

Depending on the context, practitioners may choose to give children the opportunity to share and discuss unseen worlds and in many cases this can be done naturally as part of their work. For example, what is termed 'imaginative' work is a normal part of tasks undertaken in educational settings such as nurseries, daycare centres and schools. Here, children are often asked to express their creativity and imagination through drawing, painting, model making, music, drama or creative writing. These activities, if not too highly structured, are excellent avenues for adults to give children the opportunity to express their inner worlds. Naturally, asking the child to draw or write about a magical journey through time is an exercise in imagination which is not synonymous with asking children to draw or write about a 'world' in which they necessarily believe. As such, any tasks seeking to give voice to unseen worlds need to be devised accordingly, and at the same time be structured so as not to put pressure on children to generate a world which they do not believe exists simply because an adult has asked them to present one. Many children will tell adults what they think they want to hear and if authenticity is sought, then the tasks need to be designed accordingly within the context of a safe, non-judgemental relationship.

Affirming children's worlds

Once children feel sufficiently secure in their relationship to discuss their worlds, and have granted adults access to them, adults will be placed in a position of having to respond to them. In chapter 6 some of the common responses such as 'it's just your imagination' were considered alongside the potential effects they can have on children. The following section takes a more in-depth look at why adults respond in the way they do, and how seemingly positive, encouraging responses can in fact invalidate a child's experience, particularly when they discuss their fears of darker worlds. The previous chapter invited readers to reflect on their own views about the various experiences which children have reported as well as to consider alternative explanations for them. Now, the focus moves on to encourage readers to recognise their own histories of these worlds where possible, and the responses they received so that they can become clearer about how their reactions to children have been shaped. It is acknowledged that some individuals will have stronger recall of their childhoods than others and some will remember little of their childhoods (a closer examination of memory follows in the next chapter), but even occasional memories can give insights into how we behave in the present. To aid those who remember little of their childhood worlds, examples are given to elucidate points.

Our memories and their impact on our responses

Recollections of our own childhood worlds can evoke a sense of nostalgia, a longing for the time when life was 'simple' and anything was possible; a worldview which can lie in stark contrast to the 'grown up' world of work and anxieties about how to pay the bills. Sobel (2002), when talking to adults about their childhood special places, noted that much emotion was inherent in their reminiscences. These places, often where they hid from adults and created their own private worlds, had a lasting impact on them into adulthood, when they would often mentally and/or physically return to these places with fond memories.

The nostalgia which adults may or may not feel plays an important role in their reactions to children's engagement with their multiple worlds. Tayisha, a care worker in a deprived area of London, explained,

> When a child tells me about their adventures in magical lands I often find myself welling up. It has taken me considerable time to work out why, but now I realise it's because I feel a sense of loss that that part of myself – where absolutely anything was possible – has been taken away. I guess I feel trapped by the so-called realities of life, of earning money to live and feed my child, of handling difficult colleagues, of managing personal relationships and so on. The children who attend our day centre come from deprived homes, but they seem to have this switch they can just turn on and suddenly they are transported to another realm. It has been about 45 years since I have been able to do that!

For Tayisha, who genuinely empathises with children's worlds because she recognises them as a lost part of herself, affirming children's experiences is still not necessarily easy because she finds herself emotionally affected and can struggle to express herself clearly. Yet her empathy is a significant skill which children will detect and are thus more likely to be open with her than they might with someone who is less aware or less interested in these aspects of the children's lives.

A similar story was found with Matt, who had an unusual and profound experience of seeing a city in the sky when he was nine years old (detailed in chapter 3). Matt continued to tell me how he raced indoors to tell his parents who said 'that's nice, what did it look like?' Matt ran back outside to see if he could still see it, which he could. But his parents remained in the house 'and didn't come out to validate it'. The next morning at school, during a show-and-tell session, he eagerly explained his experience to the whole class. 'And that was the most stupid thing I ever did,' he said. 'I told other people. The teacher, a nun, was very patronising and said "Oh I am sure you didn't see that."' At which point all of his classmates 'roared with laughter'. Matt said that that moment in school was 'the moment of socialisation' for him and he no longer told people of personal experiences such as this for fear of a similar response. In fact, I was the first person with whom he shared this encounter in 35 years. However, whilst the memory of being ridiculed affected him in this negative way it also had a positive impact in that he has been very open to and affirming of the narratives which his pupils have told him. He has been able to offer them a supportive ear and has been able to ensure that, at least inside his classrooms, they have been able to express themselves without fear of ridicule or dismissal.

Likewise, Marianne who described her times with her invisible companions Marjorie and Kicker in chapter 3, remains very open to unusual childhood experiences which her godson now tells her. When she was a child, Marianne had assumed that her own mother could also see Marjorie and Kicker because her mother would 'play along'. However, one day whilst playing with her invisible companions in the garden, her neighbour was watching with concern and called Marianne's mother over to suggest that the child's behaviour was not normal. Marianne's mother became worried and took her daughter to the doctor. He commented that she simply had 'a vivid imagination and that it was quite normal to have imaginary friends', a scenario that Marianne now finds quite amusing. Although Marjorie and Kicker left Marianne's life when they moved house soon after, Marianne then went on to meet an elderly lady who sat in a rocking chair in their next home. These experiences, which have remained so vivid in her memories for around 45 years, have undoubtedly made her more open to the stories of other worlds which she now hears from the young children around her.

How can adults affirm? Developing an ethos

Affirming children's experiences can be achieved in a variety of ways, both verbal and non-verbal, which will be considered here. However, any affirmation needs to be underpinned by a clear understanding of one's own perspective on the unseen worlds in order to provide a response which is grounded in integrity. It is not necessary to compromise or be unfaithful to one's own views in order to affirm children's experiences. For example, if a child claims that a ghost is throwing their toys across the bedroom, and the adult is a firm disbeliever in the supernatural, it would be insincere to respond in such a way that indicates that the adult truly believes that the ghost exists. Instead, the practitioner can respond by exploring the child's views about it, as well as alternative explanations, presented in such a way that the child can develop their own opinion in an informed way. Each situation needs to be responded to according to its individual context, but a selection of scenarios are discussed here as possible examples, and basic principles arising from them can be applied to other circumstances.

Prior to focusing more closely on specific instances, attention needs to be given to the ethos of a setting in which adults and children interact. Training for all professionals who work with children should address the ethos of their respective environment. In writing from the perspective of counselling settings, the eminent psychologist Carl Rogers identified three components of an effective person-centred relationship: acceptance, genuineness and empathy. Thorne (2002) offers a detailed overview of Rogers' many works, and summarises the above terms as follows: 'acceptance' relates to the therapist caring for the client, irrespective of the therapist's own judgements or thoughts about the client, and includes acceptance of negative thoughts as well as positive ones. Second, 'genuineness' (or congruence) refers to the therapist maintaining a sense of realness in their role rather than hiding behind a façade of the professional role; they remain transparent to the client and where necessary communicate their own thoughts and feelings, whether positive or negative. Third, empathy is vital because it allows the therapist to fully understand the ways in which the client views themselves, and allows them to enter their world without fear, but it does necessitate a high level of self awareness of one's own identity.

According to the person-centred approach, these three elements are fundamental to a positive relationship between client and therapist, and Rogers (1969, 1983) also applied his ideas to other settings such as education. He maintained that learning is far more effective when facilitative relationships are established – an idea which was then seen by many as being progressive. More recently, Pollard *et al.* (2002, p.117) apply Rogers' theory to classrooms suggesting that the acceptance pertains to receiving children 'as they are'; genuineness refers to the acceptance as being real; whilst empathy involves the teacher understanding what the classroom experience feels like to children.

In the context of schools, the ethos has long been recognised as being essential to facilitating learning and personal development. A positive and nurturing environment not only makes children feel part of a community, but also provides them with the necessary support to grow socially and emotionally. Ravet (2007) emphasises that developing and sustaining an ethos is not simply about presenting a set of values in a policy that has little bearing on the daily workings of the school. Rather, a supportive ethos leads to a setting in which rights, responsibilities, open communication and collaboration are embedded in all aspects of the institution's life. Every adult working in the school must be involved because an ethos cannot be sustained by only one or two members of staff. Simultaneously, the adults need to work as a team and respect each other because any staff tensions will be detected by children and can impact negatively on their feelings of security (Adams 2009a).

The concept of emotional intelligence plays a significant role in the developing ethos of an institution. Based on the work of Goleman (1996) who drew on that of Salovey and Mayer (1990), emotional intelligence involves five key domains:

• knowing one's emotions – being self aware and recognising emotions as they occur;

- managing emotions – being able to manage feelings in an appropriate manner;
- motivating oneself – the ability to have self control over emotions;
- recognising emotions in others – empathy;
- handling relationships – managing emotions in others is a key skill in handling effective relationships (Adams 2009a, p.37).

Weare (2004) suggests that an emotionally literate school is in part characterised by its understanding of social situations and its ability to form relationships. She argues that forming attachments to others, having empathy for them, communicating and responding effectively and managing relationships are some of the key features of such a school. Naturally, not all practitioners are emotionally literate themselves, and some have little interest in becoming so, which can create practical difficulties for those who are, when trying to create and maintain a whole-institution ethos.

Irrespective of the type of professional setting, an emotionally literate environment can impact positively on children's expression of their unseen worlds. Clearly, the high profile given to empathy is of direct and immediate benefit to children and can contribute significantly to adults understanding children more deeply. Further, the emotional components – of knowing one's emotions, managing them and managing them in others – also play an important role as children can experience strong feelings in relation to their unseen worlds. These might include, for example: fear of darker worlds; anger at people dismissing their experiences; and awe, wonder and excitement at their own experiences, such as seeing what others apparently cannot.

Is creating a supportive ethos as simple as it first appears, however? Whilst Pollard *et al.* (2002) support Rogers' theory of person-centred relationships, they caution that when it is applied to non-counselling settings, such as schools, further complications are inevitable. They argue that because teachers are obliged to ensure that children learn adequately and appropriately, this can constrain their ability to give unconditional warmth and positive regard. The need to maintain discipline, often in large groups of children, which in turn ensures that children can learn adequately and appropriately, is a major factor which affects the teachers' actions. Teachers need to balance having earned respect from the children by creating a strong ethos based on empathy with the requirement to maintain authority; a task which is inherently complex.

For all adults interacting with children, one of the key skills necessary to aid the development of emotional intelligence is the need to listen carefully in order to hear what the children are saying. In any conversation it is easy to misinterpret what another is saying for a variety of reasons including the tendency to project one's own views or perceptions on to another person.

The field of counselling has provided considerable guidance on how to listen to another person effectively, the principles of which can also be applied to non-counselling settings. Geldard (2008) describes the skill of active listening as applied to working with children in counselling scenarios, as comprising of four major components. The first is to match body language in order to indicate to the child that the counsellor is listening carefully and may include mirroring the child's body language, including matching levels of eye contact and/or matching the speed and tone of their voice. The second component is the use of minimal responses which can be non-verbal, such as a nod of the head, or short verbal comments such as 'yes' or 'okay'. By saying little, the adult is perceived to be taking a listening role. The third element is the use of reflection whereby the adult reflects on the content of what is being said through paraphrasing, and where the adult reflects on the child's feelings. (Whilst the reflection on feelings is particularly pertinent to counselling situations because it encourages the child to deal with significant emotions instead of avoiding them, adults who are not qualified counsellors should not be probing deeply into this area.) The final component is the use of summarising, by which the adult draws together the key points in the content of what the child has said, alongside reference to the feelings they have described. Summarising allows adults to be sure that they have heard what the child has said accurately and reduces the possibility of misinterpretation.

Through developing one's listening skills, adults will be able to increase their ability to hear what children are saying, which in turn will allow for greater understanding of their viewpoints. In so doing, an adult can become more proficient at understanding a child's emotional responses, thereby becoming more empathic. In order to illustrate this further, and the ways in which affirmation can be given, the following scenario is offered as an example.

Affirmation: seeing a ghost

> Charlie is seven years old and runs into the child care centre in an excitable state, shouting, 'Mrs Patel, I've just seen a ghost outside in the play area! It was a girl, she was wearing old clothes like the teacher showed us on our programme about the old days, and the girl smiled at me. She had a big hoop and a stick what she was playing with, and she held her stick out to me cos I think she wanted me to play with her, but then I looked again but she wasn't there.

Charlie had not been frightened by his encounter, in fact he was somewhat energised by it, and very open to telling the adults who were caring for him, as well as appearing to be very accepting of having seen the girl in Victorian costume. There are different ways in which Mrs Patel might affirm Charlie, irrespective of whether or not she believed that it was possible to see ghosts from the past. Here are some possible positive responses:

AN OPENING RESPONSE

> Mrs Patel is sitting down and pulls the chair next to her out so that Charlie can sit down and she says, 'Charlie, that sounds really interesting. What did she look like?'

In this case, Mrs Patel is clearly indicating to Charlie that she is genuinely interested in what he has to say. She does this in three ways. First, she uses non-verbal body language to invite Charlie to sit down next to her, which is showing him that she is offering time to listen to his story in more detail. Second, she is simultaneously making this intention explicitly clear by verbal means and third, by asking the supplementary question about what the girl looked like, she is giving Charlie the opportunity to provide more details so that she can understand his experience in more depth. The open-ended nature of the question facilitates further dialogue, which a closed question would not have done.

THE MIDDLE
The middle of the conversation will naturally depend on a variety of factors, including the nature of the relationship between adult and child, the age and maturity of the child and their willingness to disclose more information and the direction which the conversation may take. However, there are several lines of enquiry which might be appropriate and, again, the use of open-ended questions will be potentially valuable and might include some of the following:

- 'You said she looks like a girl off a television programme – can you tell me a bit more about her?'
- 'How did you feel when you saw her?'
- 'You said she had disappeared – why do you think that was?'
- 'Why do you think she wanted to play with you?'
- 'How do you think it is possible for a girl from the past to come here now?'

Questions such as these can elicit more information related to Charlie's recall of the event and also gain some insight into Charlie's understanding of it, including his own explanations for it. The questions do so without judgement. However, a conversation should not be an interrogation! The conversation should be as relaxed and informal as possible and should be at the pace of the child in question. Similarly, the questioning should not be all one way and the child should be given the opportunity to ask their own questions of the adult. Some children will want to ask, 'Have you ever seen a ghost, Miss?' or, 'Why do you think the girl was in a play area?' or, 'My mum would say it was my imagination, but what do you think?' How you answer such questions may depend on your personal views and/or the context in which you are working, but if you are ever apprehensive, you can remain neutral with answers such as, 'Some people will always think it's imagination, others will say it's not, so there is no right or wrong answer. What you think is important.'

Any questions should be interspersed with positive affirmations that indicate genuine interest, which may be short verbal comments such as, 'That's interesting', 'Okay', 'I see' or 'mmm', as well as non-verbal communications such as a smile or a nod of the head. Throughout any conversation the adult should be mindful of the fact that a child may not want to engage in any further conversation, so it is essential that the adult is not putting pressure upon them to do so. The adult needs to be sensitive to the child's responses and should detect if they are reluctant to talk or maybe using other avoidance strategies, such as fabricating details as a means of satisfying the adult.

CLOSURE

Closing a conversation with the child may not always be clear-cut because children may sometimes take the initiative, perhaps because they are bored, their attention has been taken by something else, they genuinely do not have any other information to add or they feel too pressured to be providing answers. However, any ending of such a conversation should indicate to the child that they can always return to the adult in the future if they wish to talk about this or similar experiences again.

That said, there will be occasions when children do not want to engage in a conversation about their experience. Often children, particularly younger ones, do not seek explanations or dialogue; they simply want to tell others what has happened. Young children may be more accepting of what they see or hear because they are less aware than older children of society's questioning of some types of experience. After all, until a certain point in life, we all assume that what we see and hear is the same as that which everybody else does, until we start to learn that that is not necessarily the case. Hence, older children who have come to this realisation may want to offer their own explanation for it or seek alternatives, in which cases the above questioning-orientated scenario will be applicable.

Too much affirmation?

Adults are aware of the need for children to receive affirmation in order to develop their self-esteem and practitioners are trained to give children as much encouragement and positive reinforcement as

possible, alongside constructive advice to assist them in their learning
or development. With regards to children's expression of their inner
worlds, children certainly need to feel that what they are saying is
taken seriously, but there is a potential danger of offering too much
affirmation. When writing of children's spirituality, Hart (2003) warns
that too much attention or elevation can reinforce the idea that the
child is particularly special – that they are more spiritual than others.
If adults over-emphasise children's spiritual experiences, Hart warns,
there is not only the danger of pressurising them to perform for others
to win approval, but also a danger that they are placed on a pedestal. As
a consequence, children may exaggerate or create further experiences
in order to fulfil the adult expectations or to gain approval.

Hart's advice is equally applicable to the worlds detailed in this
book, whether or not readers choose to label them as spiritual. It is,
after all, natural for children and adults alike to seek affirmation in
many things; it is not only part of creating and shaping identity but
also a way of forming relationships and making sense of our lives. Part
of that process of constructing our own identity involves responding,
consciously or unconsciously, to labels placed upon us by others. A
common example in a professional setting is a child who displays
disruptive behaviour, whom practitioners quickly label as 'naughty'.
This label is quickly used by other children who in turn go home
with tales of how 'naughty' Mark was today, and how many times he
was 'told off' by the care workers. In turn, the child's reputation can
spread quickly throughout a community and at the same time, Mark
can come to view himself as 'the naughty boy' and fulfil the role by
engaging in more of the same behaviour.

With regards to unseen worlds, similar labels and self-fulfilling
prophecies can apply. Perhaps, as Hart (2003) cautions against, a child
can be labelled as a type of mystic who can see auras or angels. In other
instances, a child who has invisible companions might be heralded as
being exceptionally gifted in imagination, or a child who sees the
'ghosts' of deceased people as being in contact with the other side.
One danger of over-affirmation is that a child can become labelled in
a way which may not be positive for them, or easy to fulfil, and as
a consequence they may begin to fabricate stories simply to satisfy
others.

Dealing with children's fears

Chapter 5 detailed children's darker worlds and their fears of them. Given that it is essential for adults to acknowledge these fears, it is also necessary to consider approaches to managing them when they are expressed. Sorin (2003) undertook a study of 45 children aged three to five years, investigating their fears, as well as their parents' and caregivers' strategies for responding to them. She suggests that whilst emotions which are deemed positive such as happiness are often encouraged in young children, other emotions such as fear are often ignored or stifled. Her analysis suggests that some common strategies inadvertently invalidate children's fears, for instance, telling a child that there is nothing to be afraid of can invalidate their feelings because it does not acknowledge them. Sorin offers the example of a father who reassured his four-year-old daughter that she would not be hurt because he had 'got hold of' her (p. 82). This approach may implicitly suggest to the child that she would not be safe on occasions when her father was not present. Another common strategy used by adults was redirecting children's attention to distract them from their fear, which Sorin suggests is inadequate because it is a temporary measure and also invalidates the child's fear because it does not address it. Consequently children may repress and internalise their fears.

How then, can adults support children who express fear of unseen worlds? When writing of fear in general, Sorin (2003) emphasises the importance of explanation and discussion in addressing them rather than avoiding them. She offers the example of a practitioner who dealt with children's fear of spiders by explaining how spiders are part of the natural world and that whilst some types are dangerous, others are not and humans need to be careful and responsible when encountering them. With reference to unseen worlds, the situation is naturally more complex because the existence of invisible companions or ghosts is dependent largely upon belief and this fact requires adults to take a more open-minded and possibly neutral approach when talking about them, as discussed below.

Sorin (2003) also proposes an approach of exploration and expression which allows children to explore the experience in more depth, including representing the fear through writing or art, or conveying it through music or drama. Such methods are particularly appropriate for supporting children's fears of nightmares, for which specific advice has been offered by various writers. For example, Siegel and Bulkeley (1998, p. 60) offer guidelines for parents/carers which include the following four points:

- First, offer a specific verbal and physical reassurance such as, 'That dream must have really worried you. Let's talk about it or draw a picture and then it won't be so scary.'

- Second, remind children that everyone, including adults, has frightening nightmares at some points in their lives.

- Third, enter into discussion as to how the frightening element of a nightmare can be tamed. If it is a monster, the child might be empowered to put the monster into a cave or wave a magic wand to make him disappear, perhaps through drawing it, or writing/ telling a story.

- Fourth, the adult and child can rehearse strategies to reduce the power of the threatening element so they might pretend to trick a monster into going into a cage, then lock the door and throw away the key so he cannot get out again.

Mallon (2002) also suggests making a 'dream catcher' which is a Native American tradition. The catcher comprises a hoop which is decorated with feathers, beads and other ornaments, and across the centre is a woven web. The dream catcher is placed in the bedroom and catches good dreams in the web whilst the bad dreams disappear through the gaps.

Sayre Wiseman (1989) conducted workshops for children in the USA, many in schools, aimed at helping children deal with their nightmares. She asks them to draw the dream, the act of which places a child in control. The child is then asked if they feel safe enough to re-enter the nightmare and if they are too frightened to recall it, she encourages them to create ways of empowering themselves. Strategies include drawing a shield, capturing the monster in a cage, creating an army of friends to help them become invisible. The next stage is to encourage the child to talk to the monster/frightening figure and ask why it has come, which gives a child authority over it. Sayre Wiseman encourages the children to try negotiating with their character rather than simply trying to kill it and focuses on creative resolutions by which children take responsibility. She details nightmares of a

12-year-old boy named Cliff who used to have nightmares about a giant ball-shaped being whom he called the Bubba Ball, which had eyes and a mouth who transported people by sucking them up and carrying them away. In his nightmare, Cliff found himself in a hot air balloon with another boy and as they went through the clouds a strong wind appeared and the Bubba Ball attacked the balloon, knocking his friend to the ground, and took Cliff away. Cliff spent considerable time trying to find a solution, initially drawing sand bags to stabilise the balloon and drawing a plane which could fly faster than the Bubba Ball could. Eventually he found a solution by going to the director of the Bubba Balls who gave Cliff a job which enabled him to make the Bubba Ball stay away for a year, whilst Cliff drew some wings as a symbol of his authority which enabled him to fly independently.

Fears of nightmares are common because they are natural phenomena which most children experience, and theories have offered explanations for them and ways in which to reduce their intensity. However, when dealing with fears of other unseen beings, such as monsters which lurk in the dark, unpleasant invisible companions or ghosts, the resolution is far less clear, because, as noted above, the very existence of entities is questioned by many who see them as the product of an over-active imagination. Yet, as already discussed, telling a child that something they fear is just their imagination is potentially damaging and dismissive of their fear. If a child appears distressed in a professional setting, it may be necessary to inform the child's parents/carers. It is important that an adult who is not a trained counsellor/therapist does not attempt any pseudo-therapeutic approaches. However, some response will be required, so what can be done?

If a child is particularly frightened by an encounter with a ghost, for example, then the adult could facilitate a conversation which considers alternative explanations for the incident. This could be done in such a way that the child offers their own thoughts on other reasons for it so that the child has some responsibility and ownership of finding reassurance. For instance, if a child suggests that it might have been their imagination, then this will have more power than an adult saying the same thing, because the latter can be perceived by the child as not acknowledging their fear.

Another approach involves taking a neutral stance but providing a wide overview of credible ideas. Essentially this includes acknowledging that people have very different understandings of the same event, and accepting that in some areas of life there are no simple right or wrong answers. It should be explained to the child that some people believe in ghosts but others do not, and that there will always be disagreement. Some people claim to have taken photographs of ghosts whilst others say they are hoaxes, there was dirt on the lens or a reflection of something material, so again we cannot be certain. If the child is genuinely frightened then a professional judgement might be made to place more emphasis on the explanations which favour the logical approach; but irrespective of choice, it is important to seek the child's views and help them find their own resolution rather than impose one on them.

Valuable resources to have on hand include books which are written for children with the express purpose of allowing them to process their fears. If there is access to a budget for books or multi-media resources, then it is very worthwhile to have a small selection on the premises so that if an unexpected conversation arises, you can have immediate access to them.

Encountering the unusual

Whilst practitioners and caregivers may hear many stories of unseen worlds, most will be familiar with many of them either because they experienced them themselves or because they are in common discourse. Occasionally, however, the more unusual scenario may arise such as a near-death experience which is less frequent and less discussed in society as a whole. The International Association for Near-Death Studies (2006) suggest that if a child reports an NDE, adults should first and foremost listen and be receptive to the child's story and help the child discern when and with whom they should discuss the experience. Of particular importance is that the adult should become knowledgeable about the phenomenon by reading around the subject; this latter point about becoming well-informed is applicable to all areas of unseen worlds with which adults are not familiar especially if they encounter similar themes from the children around them. Through education on the relevant topics, adults will be increasingly better placed to support the children with whom they work. However, the information accessed must be from reliable sources. Whilst information on all topics is available at the click of a button, or on a bookshelf in a shop, material is not necessarily accurate or based on grounded research. Where possible, seek out reputable organisations and researchers who are known in the field.

Some recommendations

- Accessing children's worlds is not necessarily straightforward. Whilst many children, especially young ones, will openly share their experiences and thoughts, older children become more selective. Ensure that you always show an open-minded attitude towards the different types of unseen worlds, even if you do not believe in the objective reality of them. Children will need to know that you will respect their comments and not judge them; taking a non-judgemental approach is key to being given access.

- Access must never be invasive. Children have the right to privacy and must always be given options not to share in such a manner that they still feel included in any conversation or activity in which they are engaged. Opt-out clauses are particularly useful in this situation. For example if a group of children are undertaking an activity in depicting a special dream, you can explain to the children that if they have not had one, or do not wish to share one, then they can create a fictional one instead. This alternative allows children to be included in the task whilst not having to identify themselves as being different from the others in the group who are choosing to share.

- Being granted access to children's worlds is a privilege particularly in view of the fact that many children, as much as they love their parents/carers, do tell researchers that they do not share such experiences with them. If a child chooses to tell you, honour that opportunity.

- Affirming children's experiences can take a variety of forms, both verbal and non-verbal, so reflect on your communication skills to ensure that you use both types to good effect.

- A sincere approach is necessary. Children will be able to detect faked sincerity which in the long term could lead to a child withholding information of this nature because they feel that you are not interested and are not taking them seriously.

- Children are quick to detect a lack of interest, however subtle it may be. A positive phrase such as 'that's lovely', could be interpreted as an offhand comment indicating lack of interest.

- Sometimes all an adult needs to do is to simply observe and listen to a child so do not feel pressurised to enter into a discussion if that is not what the child needs or wants.

- Fears need also to be affirmed. Take care not to unintentionally negate their fears; children need to have their fear acknowledged. If you do not have counselling qualifications, take time to talk about the child's fears and if appropriate, advise their parent/carer of the incident.

As the exploration of children's worlds moves towards its end, there are some key issues remaining which need to be discussed. For some readers, problems of remembering their own childhoods may exist which may limit the degree of empathy which can be achieved. The final chapter recaps on the story thus far and offers some closing advice on how empathy can be maximised as we consider the place of unseen worlds in the context of twenty-first century understandings of childhood.

CHAPTER 9

Returning to childhood

This book is nearing the end of its voyage into the worlds of childhood but there is still some important ground left to cover. The early chapters of this book charted some of the worlds which children have described to me and other researchers around the globe. The journey began with arguably the most accessible of worlds, those of fantasy and imaginative play that Western cultures deem a natural part of childhood, which are actively encouraged in professional settings that young children attend. The worlds of play are to some extent open to adults who can, when children are willing, also participate in them.

Chapters 3 and 4 moved into realms which are often less accessible to adults, some of which are potentially more challenging, not least because some are hidden from adults' view, but also because some may not have been considered seriously before. Ultimately, children may see or hear things which adults cannot. They may travel into new spaces whilst asleep or awake and whilst they can narrate these experiences to others, ultimately they remain essentially personal and subjective. However articulate a child may be, or however well they can portray an experience through other media such as drawings, it may be impossible to convey it entirely, with its full intensity, to others.

In order to avoid the misconception that children are always blissfully happy in these worlds, chapter 5 focused on the darker elements of them in order to offer readers an honest and complete overview, and avoid a biased, romanticised representation. Some of the accounts may resonate strongly with adults who have experienced similar worlds themselves and they may re-activate distant, previously forgotten memories. In some instances the children's accounts may have been met with scepticism, but others may have been more challenging in the sense that they had posed other questions: is it conceivable that an imaginary companion is not always imaginary? Can significant dreams really have more value than our society affords them? Does a near-death experience really reveal another world, or is it simply a neurological reaction which occurs when the heart stops beating?

The book moved on to consider more closely what childhood is, and how conceptions of it affect adults' reactions to children. Looking in more depth at adults' responses, chapter 7 explored the reasons behind many individuals' lack of complete acceptance of children's worlds, examining in particular the role of culture in shaping attitudes and responses. The previous chapter offered a practical focus on supporting adults in gaining access to children's worlds and how to subsequently affirm their experiences in ways which remain true to their own beliefs. Advice was also offered for those encountering children's darker worlds.

So, where next? This closing chapter raises some final issues, beginning with a closer examination of adult filters which can create barriers to remembering our own childhood, thereby limiting the degree of empathy which we can achieve. Continuing the theme of empathy, the chapter moves into a comparison of children's worlds with those of adults, asking whether or not they really are that dissimilar. Finally, the book reflects upon the importance of acknowledging children's unseen worlds, set in the context of contemporary notions about childhood in the twenty-first century in many industrialised nations.

Returning to childhood: barriers to remembering

Throughout this book there has been encouragement to recall your own childhood. At times simply reading about a child's account may have triggered a memory, just as seeing an old toy similar to one you once owned can activate forgotten memories of playing with one. At other times, the children's experiences detailed in this book may be ones that you have never considered in any depth before or have no resonance with your own experience. You may be accepting of some, whilst about others you may be more cynical.

There is no denying that remembering childhood is not an easy task. Philo (2003) acknowledges the academic argument about the extent to which the gap between adulthood and childhood can be bridged. He cites Jones (2001) who suggests that when adults' knowledge supersedes childhood, these adult filters/lenses cannot be removed to allow access back to early states. Jones further suggests that adult constructions and memories of what it was to be a child are inevitably processed through adultness. Like Philo (2003), I recognise the complications of adult filters and the impact of developing cognitive processes which can affect adults' ability to recollect childhood and I also concur with Philo when he argues that the gap between adulthood and childhood is far from unbridgeable. Given that every adult has been a child, there is, by definition, inherent potential for some level of empathy and recognition of young peoples' experiences and understanding of them.

The adult filters certainly play a significant role in shaping and reshaping memories as part of the process by which people construct their experiences. As Principe and Smith (2008) argue, individuals use their existing knowledge and beliefs to monitor and interpret their experiences and as a result, what is remembered can often contain additional and/or different information to that which actually occurred. This situation is inevitable and hence impossible to overcome. When I spoke to Scottish siblings, Shona and Iain, they simply could not agree about events which they shared when they were children. Shona distinctly remembered them playing together in a nearby field where they were convinced that over the hill lay a portal which would have taken them into another dimension. Shona had always been intrigued about travelling through it, particularly because she was unhappy at school and was seeking an escape, which was why she remembered the scenario so vividly. However, she was never quite brave enough to go down the other side of the hill even though Iain had constantly dared her to. Iain claimed to have gone through it one day and found himself in a desert but had been so afraid he came straight back.

That, at least, was Shona's recollection of events but as she told it, Iain looked mystified and laughed,

No, sis, what on earth are you talking about? You told me you
had gone through the portal and saw people dressed in Ancient
Greek clothes like you had learned about in history, and you
were so scared you'd be stuck there and wouldn't be able to
get back home that you ran down the hill screaming your
head off.

Despite continuing discussion, neither could agree on what had
actually happened. Their memories of the same scenario were quite
different, a phenomenon which is common. So why can it be difficult
to remember accurately?

Schacter (2002) identifies the various ways in which memory
malfunctions, one of which is highly pertinent to childhood
recollections: that of bias. Schacter (2002) argues that this process
tends to reflect more about what a person knows now than what
they knew at the time recalled. He draws on a variety of studies
which demonstrate that feelings in the present clearly affect how
memories from the past are recalled with the two sometimes being
difficult to separate. If the memory bias theory is applied to childhood
recollections, it may be constructive to reflect on one's current situation
and consider how that might affect the past. Schacter (2002) argues
that an individual can display a consistency bias by which they tend
to remember elements of the past as being similar to the present,
whilst at other times change bias can occur. During this latter process,
a person remembers the past as being worse than it was which creates
the perception that their current situation has improved over time.

In addition to the complexities of how memory works, other
barriers also exist, one of which is a tendency to trivialise feelings of
childhood. This is expressed in the ways in which many adults laugh at
children's understandings of the world, albeit affectionately. A father,
Janek, told me how he had comforted his daughter by telling her that
her grandma had gone to heaven. One day she was playing in the
garden and looked up at the sky thoughtfully. She then asked, 'Daddy,
if Grandma is in heaven how will she get back down again?' Janek
admitted to laughing, not because he was laughing at his daughter
of course, but because of the charm of her response and the innocent
nature of her thinking. But to the child, this is a very serious question

which also offers insights into her own worldview and indicates how she is making meaning in relation to a difficult situation.

The world is very different from the standpoint of adulthood and it can be difficult to accept that this is how we as individuals also once understood life. Worsley (2009, p.14) further suggests that adults set up a 'boundary wall around what they deem' to be their imaginary worlds of childhood because they feel that they have outgrown them. Those who do return are often considered to have never grown up properly, possibly have unresolved pathological issues, or are really sentimental. The challenge, then, is to be able to see the worlds through children's eyes, just as we may once have also seen them.

Reconnecting emotionally

The likelihood of accurately remembering a wide range of childhood events is quite low for many reasons, not least because of the complex ways in which memory works. Schacter (2002) acknowledges that suggestibility is another malfunction of memory, whereby an individual attempts to recall something that is influenced by an idea or comment made by another. Clearly, attempts to remember experiences of the unseen can be inadvertently influenced by others' recollections or something read in a book or seen on television. Psychologists have also shown that false memories of some types can be successfully implanted in people's minds, which leads to a further concern that some adults may 'remember' experiences which did not actually happen. Such difficulties are impossible to fully overcome so it is important to try not to 'force' any recollections.

However, being able to remember and retell childhood events is not necessarily the same as connecting to them emotionally. Certainly, remembering events such as, 'I distinctly recall seeing my grandfather sitting in the chair reading a book even though he had died several months before,' is an essential part of the process, but it is only the first stage. If practitioners stop at this level of recall, that of simply remembering an episode from the past, then achieving empathy with the children in their care is not going to be maximised. However, if adults can progress to a second stage – of attaining some level of emotional reconnection – no matter how slight, then the chances of achieving empathy are increased. In reality this will most likely refer to an acknowledgement of emotion, feelings or strength of belief rather than actually being able to re-experience that emotion.

Attempts to reconnect on an emotional level, or at least recognise the emotional component, are often intertwined with feelings of nostalgia and care needs to be taken in this area because it can create a distorted, idealised sense of the past. At the extreme, nostalgia can be dysfunctional if a person uses it to live in the past and fails to move on in their lives. However, Wilson's (2005) research into nostalgia suggests that it has many positive benefits, such as being able to ground a person. She argues that by remembering and reminiscing, an individual can create coherence, consistency and a sense of identity. She acknowledges that this process can lead to a re-creation of the past, but maintains that establishing the objective truth of the past is not as important as why and how nostalgia emerges. Rather, nostalgia is an important element of the creation and shaping of identity, and she suggests that the parts of the past which a person recalls and why they recall them are of particular interest.

In the context of developing empathy with children, nostalgia will naturally arise in some cases. Just as unseen worlds should not be romanticised because they also contain frightening components, adults also need to be cautious about becoming overly nostalgic about their own childhoods. Each generation seems to be prone to idealising the past, believing that many aspects of life were better previously than they are now, but some degree of objectivity is needed in order to create a balanced picture.

There is no doubt that barriers exist to remembering our own experiences of childhood and there is little that can be done to fully overcome them. However, a complementary approach is to momentarily maintain those adult lenses and identify similarities between the ways in which adults and children think, because doing so can help to bridge the gap between adulthood and childhood.

The paradox of the unseen worlds of adults and children

Thus far, this book has focused on the experiences of children, but this section explores their parallels with adults' experiences, in order to: first, elucidate the similarities and thus reduce the commonly perceived discrepancy between 'childish and adult notions'; and second, to use this argument to support older children who can struggle with the risk of being labelled 'childish'.

Many, though by no means all, of the unseen worlds described throughout the book are also reported by some adults. In fact, there is a plethora of books on phenomena detailed in the preceding chapters which relate to adults, many of which barely mention children. For example, Dash's (1997) compilation of unusual experiences is primarily focused on adults, with only a small number of young people's accounts appearing in it. Another instance is found in studies into near-death experiences which tend to be mostly associated with adults. Some books such as those by Kellehear (1996) and Moody (2001) make little reference to children's accounts at all. Whilst NDEs are obviously encountered by a very small number of people, and by no means everybody who has died and been resuscitated reports one, the International Association For Near-Death Studies (2006) makes the interesting point that with advances in resuscitation techniques, the number of NDEs is likely to increase. They contextualise this comment with regards to their research which indicates that about 85 per cent of children who suffer cardiac arrest have had an NDE. With more children surviving cardiac arrest due to enhanced medical technology, the possibilities of more young people having an NDE are growing. Hence NDEs are a phenomenon which might become more associated with children in the future.

Similarly, most studies into significant dreams are again focused on those of adults. Authors who compile overviews of significant dreams that have been reported throughout history regularly cite inspiring accounts from well-known people. These include the dream of Friedrich von Kekule, professor of chemistry in Belgium in 1854. Chemists were under pressure to identify the structure of the benzene molecule of carbon and hydrogen atoms which was impeding the progress of the science. One afternoon as Kekule fell asleep in his chair, he dreamt that atoms were juggling before his eyes, 'moving in a snake-like and twisting manner... one of the snakes got hold of its own tail and the whole structure was mockingly twisting'. When Kekule awoke he immediately realised that this image was in fact the chemical structure that had eluded scientists worldwide: it was a closed ring, rather than a straight line – with an atom of carbon and hydrogen at each point of a hexagon. This discovery of the 'benzene ring' was thus identified in a dream (Bulkeley 2000, p. 209; Adams *et al.* 2008).

Significant dreams reported by people who are not well known for reasons other than having had noteworthy dreams also appear in the literature. Kramer (2007) details the dream reported by David Booth, a 23-year-old office manager who lived in Cincinnati, Ohio, USA. In 1979, David had a recurring nightmare for ten consecutive nights in which he heard the sound of large engines failing and saw an American Airlines passenger plane swerve and roll in the air before crashing into the ground engulfed in red flames. On 22 May he made telephone calls to American Airlines, the Federal Aviation Administration (FAA) at Cincinnati airport and to a psychiatrist. The FAA took his account seriously but could not match the site to his description. Four days later on 26 May, an American Airlines DC-10 crashed at Chicago O'Hare international airport killing 275 passengers. As the FAA noted, the circumstances of the crash closely matched David's description.

Yet few overviews of significant dreams mention those reported by children, perhaps with the exception of the tragic case of Eryl Mai Jones, a ten-year-old Welsh girl who, in 1966, told her mother that she had dreamt that her school was covered in a black substance. The dream had alarmed Eryl Mai and made her frightened about going to school, but her mother insisted that she went. Two days later, Eryl Mai and 143 schoolmates died as her school in Aberfan, Wales, was buried under black coal deposits in a landslide (Van de Castle 1994, Mallon 2002, Adams *et al.* 2008).

Books describing angelic encounters also provide another example of texts which often predominantly focus upon adults' reports, such as those of Heathcote-James (2009) and Eckersley (2009). Their works, like others, narrate adults' descriptions of encounters with angels although it is interesting to note that some are recollections from childhood. On the one hand, children's encounters with unseen worlds are relatively scarce in the literature and, further, when they do exist they are often limited to specific types of studies. For example, studies of imaginary companions are usually located in developmental psychology which views them from a standpoint of how children differentiate between fantasy and reality. Yet an examination of the shelves in bookshops shows that adults' encounters of unseen worlds are more prevalent in terms of mass-market books, and tend to be labelled supernatural. Adults and children's experiences are thus often largely segregated by authors, researchers and publishers, yet bear many similarities.

Children's and adults' thinking

The range of adults' behaviours and thinking with reference to unseen worlds covers wide ground and for some goes far beyond the occasional magical or superstitious thinking when they feel out of control of a situation. For some, the 'unseen' is a part of their everyday life. Two forms of this type of thinking are considered, first, what in common terminology is often referred to as the supernatural, paranormal or New Age thinking and second, religious thinking: religious in the sense of encountering the transcendent which is not seen by others but is perceived in a religious context. (Seeing an angel may be defined as a religious encounter by one person but not by another who may see it as spiritual but with no connection to religion. Further, another person may see it as both a religious and a spiritual experience.)

Opinion polls clearly show that many adults believe in a range of supernatural phenomena such as ghosts, aliens and astrology (Gallup and Newport 1991 cited in Principe and Smith 2007). A Gallup poll in 2005 of 1002 Americans revealed that three in four believe in at least one aspect of the paranormal, with the most popular being extra sensory perception (ESP) at 41 per cent, the second being a belief that houses can be haunted (37%) and the third believing that the spirits of deceased people can return to certain places or situations (32%) (Moore 2005). In the UK, a poll of over 2000 adults in 2008 by Theos (a public theology think tank) revealed that almost one in four (39%) believe in ghosts (Theos 2009), giving a similar result to the American Gallup poll. The belief in ghosts or the spirits of deceased people can thus be shared by both adults and children alike. In this instance, there is perhaps little difference at all.

The religious and spiritual

Religious beliefs also offer similar parallels with some unseen worlds in the sense that they are concerned with aspects which may only be visible to the individual and may be inaccessible to others. A religious person may, for example, believe in a supreme deity, an afterlife, spirits or angels and may sense or experience their realities in various ways whilst an atheist stands aside asserting that they do not exist. Clearly these areas may overlap with religion according to different perceptions, but there are often grey areas. For example, seeing a deceased person may be defined as a religious experience by a member of the Christian spiritualist church, another might see it as a psychological phenomenon, being a recognised part of the grieving process and yet another person may simply view it as imagination.

However, both adults and children report religious experiences. Hay (1990, p.79) compiled a table of statistics drawn from national poll data in Britain, the USA and Australia which detailed the frequency of religious experience amongst adults. The lowest figure related to a 1962 American study which showed that 20.5 per cent of people reported a religious experience, but since then, in studies from 1966 to 1987 across all three countries, the statistics have been considerably higher, ranging from 31 per cent to 48 per cent. Children, too, also have religious experiences as Robinson (1977) and Tamminen (1994) detail. Some of these include religious dreams, which are reported in both adults and children (see Bulkeley et al. 2009).

There are, then, some parallels between adults' and children's experience of unseen worlds. In some cases these are the same experiences, whilst in others they may be similar. But are there parallels between adults' and children's thinking about unseen worlds? A spontaneous response might be 'no' but Woolley (1997), writing from a developmental psychology perspective which frames the concept in terms of the ability to distinguish between fantasy and reality, poses the question of whether or not children and adults are different types of thinkers in this respect. As detailed in chapter 7, she proposes that there is a continuum of commitment to beliefs about the world with 'real' at one end and 'unreal' at the other and a range in between. Woolley observes that children do not think along fantasy lines all of the time, but think 'fantastically' about certain things in certain situations, just as adults do. A key characteristic in adults' thinking is that resorting to magical/superstitious processes is usually accompanied by a lack of control or a perceived lack of control, such as trying to influence a game of chance or overcome illness (Woolley 1997). In a similar situation, a person who is bereaved may engage in this type of behaviour, most notably during the stage of the grieving process which gives rise to denial of the death. Here, the bereaved often enters into a bargain with a supernatural force such as God, desperately pleading that they will do anything in order to not have had the person die. Clearly adults know that the past cannot be changed, that the fatal accident cannot be 'undone', but this lack of control over the incident and the suffering experienced by the loss combine to create this type of thinking, which is often quite uncharacteristic of the individual in other circumstances.

The hidden aspects of adults' worlds

A further parallel between adults and children lies with the tendency to hide experiences with which others may not empathise. Earlier I indicated various studies which suggest that children keep many of their encounters secret for fear of ridicule, dismissal or simply not being believed (for example, Hart 2003, Scott 2004, Hay and Nye 2006, Adams *et al.* 2008). Research also suggests that many adults also keep their experiences hidden. For example, Hay (1990) conducted a national survey in Britain in 1986 in which 40 per cent of people said that they had never told anybody else about their religious/spiritual experience. Hay considers the possible explanations for this secrecy and suggests that because Western culture is rooted in scientific empiricism, many people feel embarrassed to reveal their experiences, perhaps because they regard it as a weakness or because it may challenge their own personal belief system. Further, some people may wonder if the experients are actually sane. Given that the everyday picture of reality, as determined by society, can be in conflict with a religious experience, Hay suggests that this can lead to suppression. This resulting secrecy is in turn detected by children who learn that their culture places little importance upon such phenomena and thus a cycle of secrecy is perpetuated.

Of course, not all adults keep their beliefs quiet. A high profile case in point is that of Sir Arthur Conan Doyle, creator of the Sherlock

Holmes stories. Huntingdon (1997) described how Conan Doyle suffered serious damage to his reputation, particularly after arguing for the existence of fairies. Conan Doyle championed the photographs taken by Frances Griffiths aged ten and Elsie Wright aged 16 in the Yorkshire village of Cottingley, England, in 1917. The photographs showed fairies, which they claimed were genuine. The beings in the pictures became known as the Cottingley Fairies and sparked considerable debate over their authenticity. Conan Doyle became a public supporter of them and undertook enquiries of his own which he published in the *Strand* magazine and his own book *The Coming of the Fairies*. After many years, Frances and Elsie, then in their 70s and 80s respectively, told a journalist that they made the fairies out of stiff paper and held them up with hat pins, but this confession came decades after Conan Doyle's death. Huntingdon (1997) maintains that Conan Doyle's belief in fairies had been the 'greatest blow' to his reputation.

Conan Doyle's case is one at the extreme end of the spectrum in that he was a well-known and respected person whose reputation was damaged by his personal beliefs. Because of this danger there are many adults who feel that they must keep their beliefs hidden for fear of people ridiculing them. Sophie, who works as an administrator in a large office in Manchester, commented at the end of her interview that she felt that she had engaged in a confession by sharing her experiences with me. She explained, 'If only I could progress in my career to a higher position then I would have more status and may be taken more seriously about my experiences.' Throughout our conversation she regularly said, 'I haven't told my boyfriend this... if I start to tell my colleagues I see their eyes glaze over, they think I'm mad.' The lack of acceptance of people's views which fall outside of the mainstream in any society can injure people's confidence, self-belief and identity, sometimes causing them to doubt their own experiences. Unless they meet others with similar views it is easy for people to feel isolated in the sense that they do not have people around them who fully understand them, or to whom they feel they can only reveal certain aspects of themselves.

The integral nature of unseen worlds/moving between different worlds

The unseen worlds detailed in this book are not separate worlds in children's eyes. Children do not automatically compartmentalise them, but instead freely move in and out of them. The worlds are intertwined with the one that most adults consider to be 'the real world': a paper cone is a magician's hat; the shadow in the room is either a benevolent or a frightening entity; the rustling of the trees' leaves is the sound of God whispering; the last biscuit in the tin was eaten by the friend whom no one else can see; and the gentle stroking of the forehead as the child falls asleep is the protection of their guardian angel. These worlds are not separate from that in which children eat their breakfast, go to school, sit in lessons learning how to spell or visit relatives at the weekend.

From a developmental perspective, Sharon and Woolley (2004) argue that children undergo a simultaneous development of beliefs: beliefs that are considered correct, for example that dinosaurs were real; beliefs that are considered incorrect but age appropriate, for example that Santa Claus is real; but there is also a third category in which children place fantasy figures about whom they cannot be certain whether they exist or not, yet treat them differently to real figures by assigning them characteristics and abilities which ordinary people do not have. These fantasy figures are thus 'neither unquestionably real nor pretend, but somewhere in between' (p. 308). According to Sharon and Woolley (2004), young children are in the process of actively constructing the boundary between real and fantasy entities, and have not misplaced the boundary as some psychologists might suggest.

This question of boundaries provides some interesting areas for further enquiry. The very notion of a boundary, as appearing in developmental psychology, is both helpful and unhelpful. The boundaries with regards to unseen worlds are in fact, I suggest, somewhat blurred. I am apprehensive about the often unquestioned use of the terms 'fantasy' and 'reality' in some of the academic literature in that field. In some cases, the meaning is clear, for example when children are asked to imagine a blue dog sitting in a box or to imagine that they had been at a party the previous day when they had not. But in other cases, the words 'fantasy' and 'reality' are not used with such clarity in the sense that they do not take into consideration what the children's sense of the words are.

At first glance, when adults observe children interacting with unseen worlds, the distinction between fantasy and reality might initially seem relatively obvious: the tooth fairy is not real, because it is an adult fabrication to ease children's distress of losing a tooth; the children who are playing at being pirates are not really pirates on a ship carrying a chest full of treasure, but are children engaged in make-believe. However, other aspects raise more difficult issues and adults' responses will vary in part according to their own cultural definitions of reality and their individual beliefs.

It is also important to take into account the child's understanding of whether or not something they experience is real. Certainly even very young children can distinguish between reality and fantasy in the conventional sense, for example they can be certain that there is not a green six-legged cat in the bedroom even if they are told that there is. But unseen worlds can present a more complex scenario. What is real to one person is not necessarily real to another. For example, to one adult, angels may be beings who are present alongside humans, taking forms of either people or light according to particular cultural and/ or religious definitions. However, to another person, angels simply do not exist. In this context it is not a question of who is right or wrong, but a matter of personal belief. If an individual's perception of the world includes angels, and this is important to that individual, then that is to be respected even if it conflicts with our personal worldview. Many adults have relatively fixed boundaries. For example, they may take a generally empirical, rationalist view of the world whilst simultaneously believing in an afterlife which to another logically-minded person may be a fantasy. Adults can often compartmentalise their beliefs with regards to the 'unseen', yet children's boundaries tend to be far more fluid yet nevertheless well thought out. Thus, reflecting on our own personal boundaries is important in addition to reconnecting with our own childhood beliefs in order to develop empathy.

Why take children's worlds seriously?

Finally, this chapter unpacks the answer to the question, 'why take children's worlds seriously?' particularly in societies which do not value these hidden aspects of inner life and experience. The argument is made via four key themes which are interrelated:

- concerns over children's well-being;

- the debate about the perceived 'loss of childhood';

- the impact of unseen worlds on some children;

- the potential damage to the adult–child relationship of responding negatively to their unseen worlds.

Currently, there are many concerns about the well-being of children in nations throughout the world. In addition to unacceptable levels of child poverty and mortality across the globe, there are also particular anxieties about the well-being of children in many rich nations. In 2007, UNICEF, the agency of the United Nations which works for the interests of children, published its study *Child Poverty in Perspective: An Overview of Child Well-Being in Rich Countries*. It reported on the lives and well-being of children in 21 industrialised countries, exploring six categories of well-being: the material; health and safety; education; peer and family relationships; behaviours and risks; and young people's subjective sense of their own well-being. The findings led to national headlines in rich countries which fared badly, particularly the two countries which were placed at the bottom of the table, namely the USA in twentieth place and the UK at the bottom (UNICEF 2007, p. 2). Whilst the methodologies of the UNICEF study can be critiqued, there is nevertheless an increasing awareness of the need to enhance children's well-being in some rich nations. In Australia, the term has been commonplace for some time and in England and Wales it is playing a central role in the formulation of new curricula for schools, being a prominent feature of government and independent reviews of the current curricula (see Alexander 2009, Rose 2009).

The well-being of children clearly includes a vast number of factors which are outside the remit of this book, such as those in the UNICEF survey, but the components of subjective well-being are particularly pertinent. If, for example, a child feels that they cannot confide in adults about everyday and/or significant experiences, have their fears dismissed or are ridiculed for describing them, their sense of well-being may well be affected. Yet these situations are not the foci of such internationally comparative studies, even in the categories of subjective well-being. For example, the UNICEF (2007) report used indicators of self-ratings of health, life satisfaction, the degree to which young people felt left out of things, felt awkward, felt lonely and liked school.

Integral to the concept of children's well-being for those living in some industrialised nations is the argument that many are having their childhood eroded. There is strong public perception in countries such as the UK and the USA that childhood is not as rich as it once was, and that it is being damaged and 'lost' or at least shortened. As detailed earlier, children have been increasingly driven indoors to play (Jenkinson 2001, Waller 2007, Weber and Dixon 2007) and are targeted as consumers on a daily basis (Kehily 2003, Waller 2005). Further, the tween stage is now seeing unprecedented levels of serious issues which were once the realm of adults, such as increases in mental health problems, obesity, alcohol and drug intake and sexually transmitted diseases, for example. Certainly these are very real problems which need action against, but Coster (2007) suggests that when we measure them against what childhood 'should' be, we are in fact comparing them to an idealised state of childhood which never existed – an historical concept of childhood which was inherently patriarchal and middle class. The 'loss of childhood' debate is a complex one that cannot be fully detailed here, as it includes an in-depth exploration of theoretical conceptions of childhood drawn from a wide range of disciplines. However, the notion of its demise is now set in the public psyche.

How then, do these concerns about damage to childhood relate to unseen worlds? They relate to one of the key notions of 'childhood' as a time of innocence. Here, children can engage in play and other carefree activities without the worries and strains which beset adults. The worlds of fairies, magic, time travel, imaginary companions, ghosts, Santa Claus, the tooth fairy and even the monsters hiding in the shadows of the bedroom, all have their place here, where children can believe that anything is possible. Yet children, who are co-constructors of their own childhood, face interesting contradictory messages. On the one hand, adults present them with ready-made products such as the Santa Claus and tooth fairy myths, yet may be ready to deny the existence of anything which might scare them, stating that 'ghosts don't exist, they are just in stories'. Children can struggle to make sense of such conflicting messages. Are they being told that they can believe in magical beings who bring them presents but not in beings which might scare them, such as ghosts? How do they know what is real and not real? These challenges are particularly daunting for older children who are eventually told that Santa does not exist yet still perhaps encounter seemingly inexplicable events.

Yet the unseen aspects of their lives can be very important, not least because they are integral to how they experience life. The worlds are not add-ons, they are a part of children's reality of daily and nightly life, and form a considerable part of what they understand life to be. A significant part of childhood involves exploring and negotiating one's own identity and these worlds, and children's responses to them, in part define this. For example, if a child sees their deceased grandparent and decides that it is their imagination or believes that it is the spirit of their grandparent, that response will shape their views about the afterlife accordingly. The experiences can have a long-lasting impact on a person, as the testimonies of adults in this book have demonstrated, even if they come to define them retrospectively as products of their imagination decades later. It is thus essential that children's experiences are acknowledged as being potentially meaningful to the children. Where this does not occur, this can be detrimental to children.

Adults' responses to children's unseen worlds, if explicitly negative or simply lacking in interest, can have damaging consequences for that adult–child relationship, which is exemplified by Hallowell's (2007, p. 21) narration of a woman who recalled her childhood companion named Edward. He was a very serious boy dressed in Edwardian clothes who never wanted to play, only desiring to talk about nature, science and history. The woman maintained that one day her mother found an old, wooden nib-pen on the sofa just where Edward had been sitting and asked where it had come from. 'I wanted to tell her it was Edward's, but I couldn't because I knew she'd get angry. I told her about Edward before, and she just kept telling me he didn't exist and I was to stop being silly.' Her mother eventually threw the pen on the fire and warned her daughter not to mention it to her father.

Did the mother really believe that her daughter was 'being silly'? This is debatable because this particular story has a slightly unnerving element to it, so it is more likely to be the case that the mother was simply hoping that the daughter was just being silly. Her nervousness was no doubt the cause of her dismissive response. Whilst the explanation of silliness would not account for the appearance of the pen, perhaps it was easier or more comforting for the mother to try to forget what happened; by destroying the pen and asking her daughter to take a pledge of silence so that her father would not learn about it, the mother would not have to fully confront the seemingly inexplicable appearance of an old-fashioned-pen.

However, whilst the mother's response was entirely understandable given the supernatural overtones to the story, what is of particular concern is how that response affected her daughter. It had culminated in the girl's decision to no longer share such thoughts and experiences with her mother, even though she still desired to do so. This theme, of children no longer sharing with adults who are close to them, is a recurring one in the literature and is not confined to the more unusual, perhaps paranormal, experiences such as that of the invisible Edwardian boy. Given that research suggests that many children do not share their encounters for fear of not being taken seriously (for example, Hart 2003, Scott 2004, Hay and Nye 2006, Adams *et al.* 2008), it is worrying to learn that many children feel this way. It is saddening to learn that some feel that they will not be taken seriously, and choose to remain silent on such issues for fear of being disbelieved. Further, this breakdown in communication between children and adults (often their parents/carers rather than practitioners) is one which often goes unnoticed by the adults. Such a cycle cannot be beneficial to children's well-being, so there needs to be a more positive response to children's worlds because they form such an integral part of their daily and nightly lives.

The advantages of accepting children's worlds

As the previous chapters have shown, the process of accepting children's worlds may be more difficult for some people than others, but the benefits of doing so are considerable. Practitioners can play a very important role in being a receptive and respectful listener, thereby providing a confidante for children, which they might otherwise lack, and allowing children the opportunity to express themselves should they so wish. Indeed, acceptance is essential not only if we are to avoid creating adults who are fearful of sharing their experiences with others, but also to support children's social, emotional and spiritual growth. Positive relationships with children are vital in order to maximise their potential in all aspects of their development.

The invisible companion, the monster under the bed and the deceased grandfather reading a newspaper in the armchair are as much a part of their life as talking to friends in the playground or playing with their pet dog. If adults are to fully understand children they need to be aware of the meaning that children attribute to such aspects of their life which can only be done by talking to them. It cannot be achieved by simply assuming that a child is making up stories about playing with fairies in the garden because they have read stories about the fairies and are acting them out. Certainly this will be the case for many children who may state that the fairies are in their imagination, but not for all, as some will believe that the fairies are really in the garden. The only way of being certain is to engage in meaningful discourse, which in turn strengthens the adult–child relationship. But this type of dialogue cannot be taken for granted. There is a strong climate in many sectors whereby children have an increasingly powerful voice, as detailed earlier. But children are often not enabled to express their inner or spiritual voice in societies which value the material over the non-material, because adults often do not recognise or value it, and children sense this (see Adams 2009b for an extended discussion).

Open communication in which children feel safe to share their experiences, ideas and ask questions, will only lead to more dialogue of similar quality. If children have strong self-esteem and are working in a positive climate where their opinions and views are heard, they are more likely to share their perceptions and experiences. In turn, if the adults are empathic then a positive cycle will begin to emerge. Children will be more likely to share their worlds, thus bringing them to adults' attention. In so doing, adults can in turn gain a stronger insight into them, and by being empathic, can develop their understanding of what it is like to see the worlds as they do.

Some final recommendations

- To understand children's worlds through children's eyes can be a difficult process for some adults because of the power of adult lenses which is reinforced by Western cultural beliefs. To temporarily remove these lenses necessitates an understanding of childhood both with, but also without, adult impositions. For example, the study of children's imagination and its development is vital to the field, but so, too, is the study of children's perceptions of what adults perceive to be their imagination. An invisible companion may well be, according to an adult, a product of the child's imagination, and the child may concur. But to another child, that invisible companion may well be real.

- It is essential that adults enhance their communication with children about such matters, being mindful of their own personal beliefs and how they might be unintentionally conveyed to the children.

- Be aware that adults (ourselves included!) convey many contradictory messages to children in this realm: the active promotion of the Santa/tooth fairy myths but the denial of other 'magical' entities such as ghosts and the legislative power afforded to the child's voice in terms of a range of rights, which tells children they can be heard yet they often have no outlet for an inner, spiritual voice (Adams 2009b). We are not the advertisers who sell products to children which are beyond their years, and most would not wish to deny them the Santa/tooth fairy stories, but we can give them a voice to share their experiences, fears and ideas about unseen worlds. We can also help children to realise that many adults also believe in some aspects of these worlds, thereby helping children to make sense of these contradictions as they arise.

Ultimately, every adult was once a child who to some extent engaged in at least a small number of the unseen worlds portrayed in this book. Whether these worlds are the products of children's imagination or whether some reflect other realities remains a decision for each individual reader to make, but all readers are challenged to engage with children's understandings of their travels through unseen worlds.

By understanding children's engagement with these multiple worlds, and their perceptions of them, we can increase our own understanding of children. We already know so much about children, for example about their social, physical, cognitive, psychological, emotional and moral development, that it is easy to be complacent and believe that we understand them. But adult lenses cause us to see the world(s) differently to how children do and it is too easy to assume that their experience of worlds is simply a more naive one than ours, which will 'mature' in time. In order to increase empathy with young people we need to recapture the childhood lenses we once wore, rather than impose adult lenses on our understanding of their lives. Through high quality and meaningful communication with the children in our care, we can to some extent share part of their journey with them, supporting them through encounters with the darker elements and taking pleasure in the mysterious and intriguing worlds which they weave in and out of each day; worlds which we once shared and some of which, perhaps, we still do.

References

Adams, K. (2001) 'God talks to me in my dreams: the occurrence and significance of children's dreams about God.' *International Journal of Children's Spirituality 6*, 1, 99–112.

Adams, K. (2003) 'Children's dreams: an exploration of Jung's concept of big dreams.' *International Journal of Children's Spirituality 8*, 2, 105–114.

Adams, K. (2007) 'What lies beyond? Dreams of the afterlife.' *Resource 30*, 1, 23–26.

Adams, K. (2009a) *Behaviour for Learning in the Primary School*. Exeter: Learning Matters.

Adams, K. (2009b) 'The rise of the child's voice: the silencing of the spiritual voice.' *Journal of Beliefs & Values 30*, 2, 113–122.

Adams, K. and Hyde, B. (2008) 'Children's grief dreams and the theory of spiritual intelligence.' *Dreaming 18*, 1, 58–67.

Adams, K., Hyde, B. and Woolley, R. (2008) *The Spiritual Dimension of Childhood*. London: Jessica Kingsley Publishers.

Alexander, R. (2009) (ed.) *Children, Their World, Their Education. Final Review and Report of the Cambridge Primary Review*. London: Routledge.

Ariès, P. (1960) *Centuries of Childhood*. Harmondsworth: Penguin Books.

Atwater, P. M. H. (2004) *Children's Near-Death Experiences, Some Stories*. Available from: http://www.cinemind.com/atwater/Some.html (accessed 28 April 2009).

Barrett, D. (1992) 'Through a glass darkly: images of the dead in dreams.' *Omega 24*, 97–108.

Bolton, G. (2006) *Reflective Practice: Writing and Professional Development*. London: Sage Publications.

Bouldin, P. and Pratt, C. (2001) 'The ability of children with imaginary companions to differentiate between fantasy and reality.' *British Journal of Developmental Psychology 19*, 99–114.

Bowman, C. (1998) *Children's Past Lives: How Past Life Memories Affect Your Child*. New York: Bantam Books.

Bruce, T. (2001) *Learning Through Play: Babies, Toddlers and the Foundation Years*. Abingdon: Hodder Stoughton.

Bruce, T. (2004) *Developing Learning in Early Childhood*. London: Paul Chapman Publishing.

Bulkeley, K. (2000) *Transforming Dreams: Learning Spiritual Lessons from the Dreams you Never Forget*. New York: John Wiley.

Bulkeley, K., Adams, K. and Davis, P. M. (eds) (2009) *Dreaming in Christianity and Islam: Culture, Conflict and Creativity*. New Jersey: Rutgers University Press.

Bulkeley, K., Broughton, B., Sanchez, A. and Stiller, J. (2005) 'Earliest remembered dreams.' *Dreaming 15*, 3, 205–222.

Burr, R. and Montgomery, H. (2003) 'Children and Rights.' In M. Woodhead and H. Montgomery (eds) *Understanding Childhood: An Interdisciplinary Approach*. Milton Keynes: Open University/John Wiley.

Clarke, J. (2004) 'Histories of childhood.' In D. Wyse (ed.) *Childhood Studies: An Introduction.* Malden, MA: Blackwell.

Cohen, D. (2006) *The Development of Play* 3rd ed. Hove: Routledge.

Cohen, D. and MacKeith, S. (1992) *The Development of Imagination: The Private Worlds of Children.* London: Routledge.

Coles, R. (1992) *The Spiritual Life of Children.* London: HarperCollins.

Coster, W. (2007) 'Childhood in Crisis?' In P. Zwozdiak-Myers (ed.) *Childhood and Youth Studies.* Exeter: Learning Matters.

Dash, M. (1997) *Borderlands: The Ultimate Exploration of the Unknown.* London: Random House.

Department for Education and Skills (DfES) (2004) *Every Child Matters: Change for Children.* London: DfES.

Dewey, J. (1933) *How We Think: A Restatement of the Relation of Reflective Thinking to the Educative Process.* Chicago: Henry Regnery.

Domhoff, G. W. (2001) 'A new neurocognitive theory of dreams.' *Dreaming 11,* 13–33.

Eckersley, G. S. (2009) *An Angel to Guide Me: How Angels Speak to us from Beyond.* London: Rider & Co.

Fiske, K. E. and Pillemer, D. B. (2006) 'Adult recollections of earliest childhood dreams: a cross-cultural study.' *Memory 14,* 1, 57–67.

Flanagan, O. (2000) *Dreaming Souls: Sleep, Dreams, and the Evolution of the Conscious Mind.* New York: Oxford University Press.

Foulkes, D. (1999) *Children's Dreaming and the Development of Consciousness.* Cambridge: Harvard University Press.

Freud, S. (1900/1999) *The Interpretation of Dreams.* Joyce Crick, (trans.) Oxford: Oxford University Press.

Fukuda, K. (2002) 'Most experiences of precognitive dream could be regarded as a subtype of déjà-vu experiences.' *Sleep and Hypnosis 4,* 3, 111–114.

Gabriel, N. (2005) 'Adults' concepts of childhood.' In J. Willan, R. Parker-Rees and J. Savage (eds) *Early Childhood Studies.* Exeter: Learning Matters.

Gallup, G. H. and Newport, F. (1991) 'Belief in paranormal phenomena among adult Americans.' *Skeptical Inquirer 15,* 137–146. Cited in G. Principe and E. Smith (2007) 'The tooth, the whole tooth and nothing but the tooth: how belief in the tooth fairy can engender false memories.' *Applied Cognitive Psychology.* Published online in Wiley InterScience. DOI: 10.1002/acp.1402.

Garfield, P. (1996) 'Dreams in bereavement'. In D. Barrett (ed.), *Trauma and Dreams,* pp.186–211, Cambridge, MA: Harvard University Press.

Garfield, P. (2001) *The Universal Dream Key: The 12 Most Common Dream Themes Around the World.* New York: HarperCollins.

Geldard, K. (2008) *Counselling Children: A Practical Introduction* 3rd ed. London: Sage Publications.

Goleman, D. (1996) *Emotional Intelligence. Why it can Matter More Than IQ.* London: Bloomsbury.

Greyson, B. (2006) 'Near-death experiences and spirituality.' *Zygon: Journal of Religion and Science 41,* 2, 393–414.

Gunter, B. and McAleer, J. (1997) *Children and Television.* London: Routledge.

Hallowell, M. (2007) *Invizikids: The Curious Enigma of 'Imaginary' Childhood Friends.* Loughborough: Heart of Albion Press.

Handley, G. (2005) 'Children's rights to participation.' In T. Waller (ed.) *An Introduction to Early Childhood: A Multidisciplinary Approach,* pp.1–12. London: Paul Chapman.

Harris, P. L. (2000) *The Work of the Imagination.* Oxford: Blackwell.

Hart, T. (2003) *The Secret Spiritual World of Children.* Maui: Inner Ocean.

Hartmann, E. (1996) 'Outline for a theory on the nature and functions of dreams.' In *Dreaming* 6, 2, 147–170.

Hay, D. (1985) 'Suspicion of the spiritual: teaching religion in a world of secular experience.' *British Journal of Religious Education* 7, 3, 140–147.

Hay, D. (1990) *Religious Experience Today: Studying the Facts*. London: Mowbray.

Hay, D. and Nye, R. (2006) *The Spirit of the Child*. London: Jessica Kingsley Publishers.

Heathcote-James, E. (2009) *Seeing Angels: True Contemporary Accounts of Hundreds of Angelic Experiences*. London: John Blake.

Hinnells, J. (1997) (ed.) *Dictionary of Religions*. London: Penguin Books.

Hoff, E. V. (2004) 'A friend living inside me – the forms and functions of imaginary companions.' *Imagination, Cognition and Personality* 24, 2, 151–189.

Holloway, S. and Valentine, G. (2003) *Cyberkids: Children in the Information Age*. London: RoutledgeFalmer.

Hyde, B. (2008) *Children and Spirituality: Searching for Meaning and Connectedness*. London: Jessica Kingsley.

Hufford, D. (2005) 'Sleep paralysis as spiritual experience.' *Transcultural Psychiatry* 42, 1, 11–45.

Huntingdon, T. (1997) 'The man who believed in fairies.' *Smithsonian* 28, 6, 104–113.

The International Association for Near-Death Studies (2006) *Children's Near-Death Experiences*. Available from: http://www.iands.org/nde-index/ndes/child.html (accessed 28 April 2009).

Jaffé, D. (2006) *The History of Toys from Spinning Tops to Robots*. Stroud: Sutton Publishing Ltd.

James, A., Jenks, C. and Prout, A. (2006) *Theorising Childhood*. Cambridge: Polity.

Jenkinson, S. (2001) *The Genius of Play: Celebrating the Spirit of Childhood*. Stroud: Hawthorn Press.

Jersild, A. T. and Holmes, F. B. (2007) 'Fears reported by children themselves and fears recalled by adults from childhood'. In A. T. Jersild (ed.) *Children's Fears*, pp.107–166. Columbia: Teachers' College Press, Columbia University.

Jones, O. (2001) 'Before the dark of reason: some ethical and epistemological considerations on the otherness of children.' *Ethics, Place and Environment* 4, 173–178. Cited in C. Philo (2003) 'To go back up the side hill: memories, imaginations and reveries of childhood.' *Children's Geographies* 1, 1, 9.

Jung, C. G. (1948/1960) *The Collected Works of C. G. Jung*. In R. F. C. Hull, H. Read, H. Fordham, G. Adler and W. McGuire (trans and eds) Vol. 8, London: Routledge.

Kastenbaum, R. and Fox, L. (2007) 'Do imaginary companions die? An exploratory study.' *Omega* 56, 2, 123–152.

Kehily, M. J. (2003) 'Youth cultures.' In M. J. Kehily and J. Swann (eds) *Children's Cultural Worlds*. Milton Keynes: Open University/John Wiley.

Kellehear, A. (1996) *Experiences Near Death: Beyond Medicine and Religion*. New York: Oxford University Press.

Kimmins, C. W. (1931) 'Children's dreams.' In S. G. M. Lee and A. R. Mayes (eds) (1973) *Dreams and Dreaming: Selected Readings*, pp.83–109. Aylesbury: Penguin Books.

Klein, R. (2003) *We Want our Say: Children as Active Participants in Their Education*. Stoke on Trent: Trentham Books.

Kramer, M. (2007) *The Dream Experience: A Systematic Exploration*. New York: Routledge.

Lewis, C. S. and Baynes, P. (2006) *The Complete Chronicles of Narnia*. London: Harper Collins Children's Books.

Lindon, J. (2001) *Understanding Children's Play*. Cheltenham: Nelson Thornes Ltd.

Lohmann, R. I. (2001) 'The role of dreams in religious enculturation among the Asabano of Papua New Guinea.' In K. Bulkeley (ed.) *Dreams: A Reader on the Religious, Cultural and Psychological Dimensions of Dreaming*. New York: Palgrave.

Loughran, J. (2002) 'Effective reflective practice: in search of meaning in learning about teaching.' *Journal of Teacher Education 53*, 1, 33–43.

Mallon, B. (1989) *Children Dreaming*. London: Penguin.

Mallon, B. (2002) *Dream Time with Children: Learning to Dream, Dreaming to Learn*. London: Jessica Kingsley Publishers.

McKee, D. (2009) *The Extraordinary Adventures of Mr Benn*. London: Hodder Children's Books.

McLaughlin, C., Carnell, M. and Blount, L. (1999) 'Children as teachers: learning to listen to children in education.' In P. Milner and B. Carolin (eds) *Time to Listen to Children: Personal and Professional Communication*, pp.97–111. London: Routledge.

Moody, R. (2001) *Life After Life*. London: Rider.

Mooney, C. G. (2000) *Theories of Childhood: An Introduction to Dewey, Montessori, Erikson, Piaget and Vygotsky*. St Paul, MN: Redleaf.

Moore, D. (2005) 'Three in four Americans believe in paranormal.' at http://www.gallup.com/poll/16915/Three-Four-Americans-Believe-Paranormal.aspx (accessed on 25 May 2009).

Morris, R. and Kratochwill, T. (1983) *Treating Children's Fears and Phobias*. New York: Pergamon Press.

Morse, M. (2001) 'Preface'. In R. Moody *Life After Life*. London: Rider.

Morse, M. and Perry, P. (1990) *Closer to the Light: Learning from the Near-Death Experiences of Children*. New York: Villard Books.

Newcomb, J. (2008) *Angel Kids: Enchanting Stories of True-Life Guardian Angels and 'Sixth-Sense' Abilities in Children*. London: Hay House.

Papatheodorou, T. and Gill, J. (2002) 'Father Christmas: just a story?' *International Journal of Children's Spirituality 7*, 3, 329–344.

Parker, J. and Blackmore, S. (2002) 'Comparing the content of sleep paralysis and dream reports.' *Dreaming 12*, 1, 45–59.

Parker-Rees, R. (2005) 'Developing communication: enjoying the company of other people.' In J. Willan, R. Parker-Rees and J. Savage (eds) *Early Childhood Studies*. Exeter: Learning Matters.

Philo, C. (2003) 'To go back up the side hill: memories, imaginations and reveries of childhood'. *Children's Geographies 1*, 1, 7–23.

Piaget, J. (1929/1971) *The Child's Conception of the World*. Joan Tomlinson and Andrew Tomlinson (trans.), St Albans: Granada Publications.

Piaget, J. (1951/1972) *Play, Dreams and Imitation in Childhood*. C. Gattegno and F. M. Hodgson (trans and eds) London: Routledge & Kegan Paul Ltd.

Pollard, A., Collins, J., Simco, N., Swaffield, S., Warin, J., Warwick, P. and Maddock. M. (2002) *Reflective Teaching: Evidence-Informed Professional Practice*. London: Continuum.

Principe, G. and Smith, E. (2007) 'The tooth, the whole tooth and nothing but the tooth: how belief in the tooth fairy can engender false memories.' *Applied Cognitive Psychology*. Published online in Wiley InterScience. DOI: 10.1002/acp.1402.

Principe, G. and Smith, E. (2008) 'Seeing things unseen: fantasy beliefs and false reports.' *Journal of Cognition and Development 9*, 89–111.

Punamäki, Raija-Leena (1999) 'The role of culture, violence, and personal factors affecting dream content.' *Journal of Cross Cultural Psychology 29*, 2, 320–342.

Punch, S. (2000) 'Children's strategies for creating playspaces: negotiating independence in rural Bolivia.' In S. Holloway and G. Valentine (eds) *Children's Geographies: Playing, Living, Learning*. pp.48–62. London: Routledge.

Ravet, J. (2007) *Are we Listening? Making Sense of Classroom Behaviour with Pupils and Parents*. Stoke on Trent: Trentham.

Resnick, J., Stickgold, R., Rittenhouse, C. and Hobson, J. A. (1994) 'Self-representation and bizarreness in children's dream reports collected in the home setting.' *Consciousness and*

Cognition 3, 1, 30–45.

Robinson, E. (1977) *The Original Vision.* Manchester College, Oxford: The Religious Experience Research Unit.

Rogers, C. (1969) *Freedom to Learn.* Columbus Ohio: Charles E. Merrill Publishing Company.

Rogers, C. (1983) *Freedom to Learn for the 80s.* Columbus Ohio: Charles E. Merrill Publishing Company.

Rose, J. (2009) *Independent Review of the Primary Curriculum: Final Report.* Nottingham: Department for Children, School and Families.

Rudduck, J. and Flutter, J. (2000) 'Pupil participation and pupil perspective: carving a new order of experience.' *Cambridge Journal of Education 30*, 75–89.

Salovey, P. and Mayer, J. D. (1990) 'Emotional intelligence.' *Imagination, Cognition and Personality 9*, 3, 185–211.

Sayre Wiseman, A. (1989) *Nightmare Help: A Guide for Parents and Teachers.* Berkeley: Ten Speed Press.

Schacter, D. (2002) *The Seven Sins of Memory: How the Mind Forgets and Remembers.* Boston, MA: Houghton Mifflin Harcourt.

Schön, D. (1983) *Educating the Reflective Practitioner.* San Francisco: Jossey Bass.

Scott, D. (2004) 'Retrospective spiritual narratives: exploring recalled childhood and adolescent spiritual experiences.' *International Journal of Children's Spirituality 9*, 1, 67–79.

Seiffge-Krenke, I. (1993) 'Close friendship and imaginary companions in adolescence.' In B. Laursen (ed.) *Close Friendships in Adolescence.* San Francisco: Jossey Bass. Cited in M. Taylor (1999) *Imaginary Companions and the Children Who Create Them.* New York: Oxford University Press.

Sharon, T. and Woolley, J. (2004) 'Do monsters dream? Young children's understanding of the fantasy/reality distinction.' *British Journal of Developmental Psychology 22*, 293–310.

Siegel, A. and Bulkeley, K. (1998) *Dreamcatching: Every Parent's Guide to Exploring and Understanding Children's Dreams and Nightmares.* New York: Three Rivers Press.

Singer, D. and Singer, J. (1990) *The House of Make Believe: Play and the Developing Imagination.* Cambridge, MA: Harvard University Press.

Sobel, D. (2002) *Children's Special Places: Exploring the Role of Forts, Dens, and Bush Houses in Middle Childhood.* Detroit: Wayne State University Press.

Sorin, R. (2003) 'Validating young children's feelings and experiences of fear.' *Contemporary Issues in Early Childhood 4*, 1, 80–89.

Stainton Rogers, W. (2003) 'What is a child?' In M. Woodhead and H. Montgomery (eds) *Understanding Childhood: An Interdisciplinary Approach.* Milton Keynes: Open University/John Wiley.

Stevenson, I. (1987) *Children who Remember Previous Lives. A Question of Reincarnation.* Charlottesville: The University Press of Virginia.

Stewart, W. (2009) 'Union: pupil voice is used to target teachers.' *Times Educational Supplement,* 16 January. http://www.tes.co.uk/article.aspx?storycode=6007201 (accessed 7 February 2009).

Strauch, I. and Lederbogen, S. (1999) 'The home dreams and waking fantasies of boys and girls ages 9–15: a longitudinal study.' *Dreaming 9*, 2/3, 153–161.

Subbotsky, E. (1984) 'Preschool children's perception of unusual phenomena.' *Soviet Psychology 14*, 17–31. Cited in P. Bouldin and C. Pratt (2001) 'The ability of children with imaginary companions to differentiate between fantasy and reality.' *British Journal of Developmental Psychology 19*, 100.

Szpakowska, K. (2001) 'Through the looking glass: dreams in Ancient Egypt.' In K. Bulkeley (ed.) *Dreams: A Reader on the Religious, Cultural and Psychological Dimensions of Dreaming.* New York: Palgrave.

Tamminen, K. (1994) 'Religious experiences in childhood and adolescence: a viewpoint of religious development between the ages of 7 and 20.' *International Journal for the Psychology of Religion 4*, 61–85.

Taylor, M. (1999) *Imaginary Companions and the Children Who Create Them*. New York: Oxford University Press.

Taylor, J. and Woods, M. (eds) (2005) *Early Childhood Studies: An Holistic Introduction*. London: Hodder Arnold.

Theos (a public theology think tank) (2009) 'Four in ten people believe in ghosts.' http://www.theosthinktank.co.uk/Four_in_ten_people_believe_in_ghosts.aspx?ArticleID=3015&PageID=14&RefPageID=5 (accessed on 28 May 2009).

Thorne, B. (2002) *Carl Rogers*. London: Sage.

Thurtle, V. (2005) 'The child in society.' In J. Taylor and M. Woods (eds) *Early Childhood Studies: An Holistic Introduction*. London: Hodder Arnold.

Training and Development Agency for Schools (TDA) (2008) *Professional Standards for Qualified Teacher Status and Requirements for Initial Teacher Training*. London: TDA. http://www.tda.gov.uk/upload/resources/pdf/p/professional_standards_2008.pdf (accessed on 8 October 2009).

UNICEF (2007) *Child Poverty in Perspective: An Overview of Child Well-Being in Rich Countries*. Florence: UNICEF Innocenti Research Centre.

Van de Castle, R. (1994) *Our Dreaming Mind*. New York: Random House

Veen, W. and Vrakking, B. (2006) *Homo Zappiens: Growing up in a Digital Age*. London: Network Continuum Education.

Waller, T. (2005) 'Contemporary theories and children's lives.' In T. Waller (ed.) *An Introduction to Early Childhood: A Multidisciplinary Approach*. London: Paul Chapman.

Waller, T. (2007) 'The trampoline tree and the swamp monster with 18 heads: outdoor play in the foundation stage and foundation phase.' *Education 3–13 35*, 4, 393–407.

Weare, K. (2004) *Developing the Emotionally Literate School*. London: Paul Chapman.

Weber, S. and Dixon, S. (2007) *Growing up Online: Young People and Digital Technologies*. New York: Palgrave Macmillan.

Willan, J., Parker-Rees, R. and Savage, J. (2005) (eds) *Early Childhood Studies*. Exeter: Learning Matters.

Wilson, J. (2005) *Nostalgia: Sanctuary of Meaning*. Lewisburg: Bucknell University Press.

Woolley, J. (1997) 'Thinking about fantasy: are children fundamentally different thinkers and believers from adults?' *Child Development 68*, 6, 991–1011.

Woolley, J. and Wellman, H. (1992) 'Children's conceptions of dreams.' *Cognitive Development 7*, 365–380.

World Health Organisation (WHO) (2007) The World Health Organisation. *Health Status: Mortality*. http://www.who.int/en/ (accessed 14 July 2007).

Worsley, H. (2009) *A Child Sees God: Children Talk about Bible Stories*. London: Jessica Kingsley Publishers.

Wyse, D. (2004) *Childhood Studies: An Introduction*. Oxford: Blackwell Publishing.

Index

405351

Lightning Source UK Ltd.
Milton Keynes UK
21 January 2011

166125UK00001B/53/P

9 781849 050517